Printed in the United States of America

First Publishing, 2025

ISBN 978-1-7354528-0-7

Special thanks to my Lord
and Savior Jesus Christ
The insights found within this book
could not have been made without Him.

TABLE OF CONTENTS

INTRODUCTION

DIAGNOSING THE PROBLEM

"...FOR THE WAYS OF MAN ARE BEFORE THE EYES
OF THE LORD AND HE PONDERS ALL HIS PATHS. HIS
OWN INIQUITIES ENTRAP THE WICKED MAN, AND HE IS
CAUGHT IN THE CHORDS OF HIS SIN. HE SHALL DIE
FOR LACK OF INSTRUCTION"
PROV 5:21-23, NKJV

A guy suffering from the real-life consequences of a porn addiction wants to know how to stop. The physical action of stopping may be as simple as turning off the phone, computer, or television set. Yet, he cannot bring himself to do it. Inward desires strip him of the willpower to make such a choice. His heart is drawn to pornography; the graphic visuals tug at his heartstrings. He can feel it inside. Witnessing those naked women in their full glory has stimulated all his emotional buttons.

He can't get enough of them. The euphoric experience has gotten under his skin. The desire to watch has entrenched itself and is beginning to crowd everything else out. A guy may know the practice is not good. He may realize the habit is destroying his life. He just can't seem to break free of it. He is trapped by his own dark desires. As he struggles to cope, the urge to look only gains a tighter grip.

> "...THEY STUMBLED AT THAT STUMBLING STONE."
> ROM 9:32, NKJV

How does a man abstain from pornography when the desire to look constantly pulls at him? How can he overcome this emotional contagion? If a man tries to suppress his feelings, the less he will want to. This lack of incentive will only make for a half-hearted attempt. Knowing what to do is not the same thing as feeling like doing it. Before long, the addictive urges chip away at his resolve to stop and the man finds himself being pulled once again in the wrong direction. As those feelings get the best of him, the habit resurfaces. The root problem lies within. A man can't go where his heart won't follow. He can't bring himself to do what he does not have in him. Before a man can really win, something inside must change.

> "...BE TRANSFORMED BY THE RENEWING OF YOUR
> MIND."
> ROM 12:2 NKJV

The mind and heart remain a man's biggest sex organs; these two things fuel every sexual impulse of his body. Anyone who has ever said 'that turns me on' or 'that turns me off' express this dynamic. Sexual desires are the product of thinking. If a man really wants to break up a desire's stranglehold on his life, he must undercut those thoughts fueling his feelings. This will require some digging and some self-reflection on his part. A man must come to see for himself why he desires porn so much. He must clearly understand what it is he hopes to gain from watching it. Seeing and understanding how those addictive urges took shape are the key to overcoming them. A hard look must be taken at what is really wanted and why.

> "...HIS ENEMY CAME AND PLANTED WEEDS AMONG THE WHEAT, THEN SLIPPED AWAY..."
> MT 13:25, NLT

The porn viewer doesn't see the invisible forces influencing his outlook. He doesn't know where his own desires are leading him and how it will become his own undoing. Rose-colored glasses have rendered him incapable of understanding his own thoughts and feelings. Under the trance of porn's entertainment, a viewer doesn't notice all the psychological programming going on behind the scenes. Porn's messaging bypasses his head and captivates his heart. Researchers have discovered that pornography literally rewires a viewer's neural pathways. This psychological programming hijacks his brain's reward system and closes it off to every other stimulus. It should not be surprising then that a man might begin to fixate over porn. The viewer truly does not understand what has been implanted deep within his own gray matter.

> "ABOVE ALL ELSE, GUARD YOUR HEART,
> FOR EVERYTHING YOU DO FLOWS FROM IT."
> PROV 4:23, NIV

The way pornography toys with a man's emotions is truly a wicked thing. Porn producers understand male desire. Their psychological insight gives them an ability to write scripts that tap into a man's deepest feelings. These images are known to activate the same pleasure centers within the brain that any psychedelic drug might stimulate (Love, 2015) [1-3]. It gets the man's heart thumping. This ability to evoke emotion like this wields for the porn producer an uncanny level of influence and control over their audiences. It gives them an ability to captivate the whole man. Even a single exposure has been shown to be habit forming. (DeSousa, 2017) To dabble with pornography is to play a dangerous game. A guy who has never seen these visuals before will not appreciate what he is dealing with. Therefore, he will not take the appropriate measures to protect his heart from it. The average guy is not in touch with his own emotions; he is in over his head. He will think he can always walk away; but he will soon discover that he can't. Being oblivious will make him susceptible to falling under porn's spell.

" ...BUT YOU SAID, 'IT IS HOPELESS. NO! FOR I
HAVE LOVED STRANGERS, AND I WILL WALK AFTER
THEM."
JER 2:25, ESV

Why is having the wrong desires such a dangerous thing? Because desires script a man's choices and predetermine his life trajectory. Head knowledge alone cannot dispel this emotional draw. A man could be given all the superficial reasons why he should quit. His logical mind may even agree with all these reasons. Yet none of these persuasions are enough to dissuade his heart. Ultimately, a man must always go after what he loves. His choices are always restricted by his own affections; they are never random. In the long run, a man can do no other. For to an addict, the giving up of porn is equated with the giving up of pleasure itself. This idea is what keeps him bound. The mental connection between pornography and pleasure is what keeps him from seeing the answer.

> "YOU ARE NOT RESTRICTED BY US,
> BUT YOU ARE RESTRICTED BY YOUR OWN
> AFFECTIONS."
> II Cor 6:12 NKJV

The road to victory will require one's own desires be set straight. This means digging away at the misperceptions so that the incessant urges can be shaken out. Sexual feelings can only be sorted out at the desire level. Afterall, desire is what put a man into this addictive stranglehold, and it is only desire that can get him out. Nothing short of this will do. Desires are the compass needle charting a man's course. It would be wise for a man to see which direction that internal compass needle is pointing. To assess whether he really wants what he thinks he does- to course correct if needed. Desires can show a man where his own life is headed. This roadmap of things to come can be read like a spiritual blueprint. Seeing the blueprint in advance is what enables a man to make informed choices and to achieve success.

For if left unchanged, those desires written there will only play out to their logical conclusion. Ultimately, a man's desires determine his destiny. Personal transformation is the only way a man can be saved from himself.

CURIOSITY

WHY PEOPLE GET IN TROUBLE

"...O SHULAMITE, RETURN, RETURN, THAT WE MAY
LOOK UPON YOU!"
SONGS 6:13, NKJV

All human beings are curious about sex. This
curiosity often gets many of them into trouble.
Young men have budding hormones and a keen
interest in females. There is nothing wrong with
these natural desires. God made people sexual
beings. The desire to reproduce is part of being a
man. It shouldn't surprise anyone then that
pornography might be a temptation for the
average guy. Porn offers the male viewer a
window into the world of naked women and sex.
What boy wouldn't want to peer into that
window. Afterall, women are the desire of his

eyes and those pornographic images give him an eyeful.

> "WHATEVER MY EYES DESIRED I DID NOT KEEP FROM THEM…"
> ECC 2:10, NKJV

If a beautiful girl in revealing clothing walks around the corner, the average guy will want to peek at her. How much more then will his eyes be drawn to a pornographic image that shows him everything. Most boys wonder what the opposite sex looks like naked. Statistics show that this curiosity is getting the best of people. Research groups estimate 91.5% of men and 60.2% of women have watched porn before (Solano, 2020)[4]. This should not be surprising. For a guy, looking is the path of least resistance. If a man is to ever control his own natural inclinations, he must be given solid reasons for doing so; otherwise, he won't.

11

"[WISDOM WILL] DELIVER YOU FROM THE IMMORAL WOMAN"
PROV 2:16, NKJV

In Scripture, God warns people not to look, but the message is not being disseminated much. Nobody wants to tell young people like it is. Parents don't like talking to their kids about sex. Many may feel inadequate to teach on the subject; perhaps their parents did not teach them either. Religious leaders too often dance around the issue. Preferring to issue prohibitions without providing any explanation as to why. Few clergymen want to elaborate in any kind of detail. The topic of sex can be messy and uncomfortable to talk about. The fear of looking bad makes it hard to have any candid discussion about the subject. In such an environment, how is a young person supposed to be equipped with the spiritual resources needed to resist such temptation?

> "WOUNDS FROM A FRIEND CAN BE TRUSTED,
> BUT AN ENEMY MULTIPLIES KISSES."
> PROV 27:6, NIV

A kid can't be expected to refrain without a proper explanation. The admonition to go without porn will only be perceived as trying to hide something wonderful from them. A young person does not appreciate the consequences of looking. Naivete keeps them from fully appreciating the dangers. A young person need straight answers. Otherwise, the culture will succumb to these encroaching influences. Whenever parents and churches take the "hands-off" approach to this subject, they are abdicating their teaching role to the porn industry. Porn will show a kid everything about sex a parent won't.

"THE ROD OF CORRECTION IMPARTS WISDOM, BUT
A CHILD LEFT TO HIMSELF DISGRACES HIS MOTHER."
PROV 29:15, NIV

A parent cannot shield their child from this
influence anymore. The culture is bombarded
with these sexual images every day. A child will
have no difficulty in finding these images. In the
age of cell phones, pornography is everywhere
and is often free of charge. With the introduction
of the smartphone, children's exposure to porn
grew from 14% to 49%. Statistics say seven out
of ten kids will stumble upon the material
accidentally. Three out of ten will deliberately
seek it out after learning about it from their
friends. For the average boy, this initial exposure
is said to occur between the ages of 8 and 11. The
porn narrative undermines everything parents and
churches try to teach their kids. It perverts a
child's impressionable mind and strips him of his
innocence. This indoctrination often occurs right

under a parent's nose. Ultimately, a kid will follow whatever he comes to glorify. When he becomes of age, he will seek to reenact those things that have been engrained into him.

"DISCIPLINE YOUR SON, FOR IN THAT THERE IS HOPE; DO NOT BE A WILLING PARTY TO HIS DEATH."
PROV 19:18, NIV

Pornography's influence in the culture is growing like a weed. The average internet user is said to spend about 40% of their waking hours on-line (Reportal, 2020) [6]. Out of all this viewing time, 35% of the internet traffic is said to be pornographic and 25% of all the search requests will be porn related (Dines, 2011) [7]. A 2021 Survey has shown several viewers credit pornography with everything they know about sex. One in four have had no other mentor (Rothman, 2021) [5]. These statistics makes a clear statement. Porn is winning the culture war. Political correctness is impairing the culture's ability to fight this scourge.

"TRAIN A CHILD IN THE WAY HE SHOULD GO, AND WHEN HE IS OLD HE WILL NOT TURN FROM IT."
PROV 22:6, NIV

Clearly, the "hands off" approach does not work. At present, churches are losing the battle for hearts and minds. As a result, real people are suffering the consequences. Secular message boards have cropped up all over the internet detailing people's devastating experiences with pornography. Anti-porn websites are filled with these sad accounts of personal lives that have been destroyed. A person could learn from these mistakes. They don't have to learn these lessons the hard way. Heeding the warnings and possessing a healthy fear of these things could keep people safe. If parents and churches really want to inoculate their children from these encroaching influences, those underlying heart issues must be addressed. The problem of porn must be dealt with head on. This means teaching our kids about things a person may feel uncomfortable discussing.

HORMONES

THE DANGERS OF PLAYING WITH FIRE

*"THEN GOD SAW EVERYTHING THAT HE HAD MADE,
AND INDEED IT WAS VERY GOOD…"*
GEN 1:31, NKJV

A man doesn't have to feel bad about desiring women or wanting to have sex with them. God created those sexual hormones within a man. He created sex and it's pleasures to incentivize people to multiply on the earth (Gen 1:28). In the beginning, God presented the woman completely naked to the man and told them to be fruitful and multiply. The two became one flesh and were not ashamed (Gen 2:22-25). This kind of sex was not sinful; everything God made He called good

(Gen 1:31). A married couple doesn't have to feel guilty over enjoying sex. The sexual pleasures shared between a husband and a wife stimulate lovemaking. These powerful feelings bond a man and a woman together. The precedent to create love and children in the same act was set at creation. Lovemaking creates the perfect environment for a child to grow up in. Children raised in a loving home make the world a better place.

> "ALSO FOR ADAM AND HIS WIFE THE LORD GOD MADE TUNICS OF SKIN, AND CLOTHED THEM."
> GEN 3:21, NKJV

In their proper place, sex can be a wonderful thing; but it can also become a terrible thing when mishandled. The good thing God made can be used to create havoc. Immorality can ruin a person's sex life. God is not against sex but sexual immorality. When sin entered the world, Adam and Eve were given clothes. These clothes were given to them as a safeguard against immoral behavior. If a man really wants to have a great sex life, the propensity to behave immoral must be avoided. This primary safeguard involves limiting what a man can see.

"... [LOVE'S] FLAMES ARE FLAMES OF FIRE, A MOST VEHEMENT FLAME."
SONGS 8:6, NKJV

The Bible equates the hormonal passions within a man and a woman to a fire. Sexual fires can be good. These kinds of fires will keep a married couple warm at night. But in the wrong place, these same powerful feelings can burn everything to the ground. Therefore, precautions must always be taken in handling these fires. The male heart is a regular tinderbox of passionate emotion. These fiery passions are easily ignited at the sight of a beautiful naked woman. If man really wants to have a good sex life, then he must control what he looks at.

"...THE FIRE NEVER SAYS ENOUGH"
PROV 30:16 NKJV

The guy who dabbles with porn is playing with fire. He thinks looking will somehow quench his burning itch to see. Flipping through that stack of girlie magazines, watching those porn videos, or frequenting the strip clubs will never alleviate a man's burning itch to look; these activities will only intensify the urges. Staring fans the flames; it only makes the burning worse. Understand a fire never says enough. The more a guy looks at these things, the more he will want them and burn inside. Guys get burned all the time looking at pornography. That painful burning is the first natural consequence of looking; a spiritual foretaste of what awaits those who disobey God.

21

"THEY PREPARE THEIR HEART LIKE AN OVEN…"
HOSEA 7:6, NKJV

For a man, the only safe way to put out those burning feelings is to stop looking. For all their fury, hormones do need fuel to keep going. Even the strongest fires will die out without any fuel to sustain them. Stop feeding the fire and let it die down. The best time to stop is always now. Small sparks and embers are manageable and relatively easy to extinguish. The task will only get harder as time goes on. Looking away and putting those images out of one's mind minimizes the emotional and physical damage. A man will only compound his losses if he delays. If he allows those desires to burn uncontrolled, he will enter into peril.

> "...SEE HOW GREAT A FOREST A LITTLE FIRE KINDLES!"
> JAMES 3:5, NKJV

Those small hormonal sparks can grow into immense firestorms. Hormones that are allowed to burn too hot will flash over and cause everything to go up in flames. A point of no return does exist when coming back from the brink is no longer possible- when consuming emotions sabotage every common-sense faculty. In these moments, the man on fire will lose his head; raging hormones will overpower his ability to think. He will begin to make some very foolish decisions. He will act wickedly and not think twice about it. The emotional fog that comes over him will carry him to places he never intended to go. His irrational exuberance will burn everything to the ground. Consequences will not stop the man overcome with these emotions.

Sexual passions are a very powerful thing; they are even stronger than the fear of death. The threat of death will no longer intimidate such a person. This is why playing with hormones can be so hazardous. Emotions move people more than anything else. Their ability to get the best of a person adds a real element of danger.

> "... FOR LOVE IS AS STRONG AS DEATH, JEALOUSY AS CRUEL AS THE GRAVE..."
> SONGS 8:6, NKJV

When these fires exact a painful toll, onlookers can only stand by and witness the carnage. After the dust settles, the man on fire will come to regret his choices (if he survives).

In the wake of such destruction, outsiders will marvel at the man's own stupidity and why he lets his feelings rage out of control. Bystanders don't see themselves as making the same mistakes; they like to think of themselves as smarter than that.

Such overconfidence leaves them vulnerable to making the same mistakes. Outsiders forget those same hormones also reside within them. The same tinder box of emotion lies dormant in everyone. Hormones that lie dormant for long periods are sometimes believed not to exist.

> "DO YOU SUPPOSE THAT THESE GALILIANS WERE WORSE SINNERS THAN ALL OTHER GALILIANS, BECAUSE THEY SUFFERED THESE THINGS? I TELL YOU NO; BUT UNLESS YOU REPENT, YOU WILL ALL LIKEWISE PERISH."
> LUKE 13:3, NKJV

The onlooker doesn't appreciate how those fiery passions could make him feel inside should they be awakened. He underestimates what these feelings could make him do. Know that overconfidence got that "stupid" man into his mess. His curiosity and carelessness made him reckless. He dabbled in porn and did not flee the danger when the opportunity presented itself. By underestimating porn's ability to light his fire, he got in over his head. He got burned thinking he could handle it. He didn't know 'the point of no return' line had been crossed until it was too late.

NUDITY

"FOR AS HE THINKS IN HIS HEART, SO IS HE."
PROV 23:7, NKJV

The average guy sees little harm in staring at pornography. The act of looking is considered a private affair- a personal matter of the heart. What does it matter if a man stares at a naked woman on the screen? Nobody will be able to see what goes on within his heart. If he has impure thoughts about a woman, she will not be able to read his mind. If nobody else knows, then nobody else is hurt by it- right? This is how the thinking goes. The man thinks nobody else can see him. Because merely looking at a woman doesn't appear to hurt anyone else, the musings of one's heart are considered to hold no consequence. So long as a man does not touch the woman, he will feel like he can look to his heart's content. A man will often tell himself: 'I can look so long as I don't touch.'

"WHOEVER LOOKS AT A WOMAN TO LUST FOR HER HAS ALREADY COMMITTED ADULTERY WITH HER IN HIS HEART."
MATT 5:28, NKJV

This peeking behavior seems innocent until a person begins to delve below the surface. The voyeur is doing more than just observing someone; he is visualizing a lot more than what is there. He is fantasizing about the possibilities within his mind. He is imagining himself being with the woman and doing things to her. His dirty mind fills in a lot of details with the wildest of notions. The voyeur doesn't see anything wrong with this. Those inner musings are never

28

seen as something bad. When he looks past a woman's clothes to behold what lies underneath, he does not see it as an invasion of her privacy. When he imagines himself making love to her without her consent, he does not see it as a form of adultery or rape - even if his heart is in the same place. To the average guy, the inward thought is not the same as the outward deed.

> "... THE EYE NEVER HAS ENOUGH OF SEEING..."
> ECC 1:8, NIV

A guy may look at porn to satisfy his curiosity, but he will never be satisfied with what he sees. His eyes could never see enough of it. A man who looks at porn does not see the folly of his way. He doesn't understand that looking can become a slippery slope. He could devour a myriad of these images; staring at everything his heart might wish to see will never leave him satisfied. A man is a visual creature; his sexual hormones are only triggered by those beautiful naked women on the screen. Before long, he will want to touch those women on the pages of a porn magazine; know the desire to look will always turn into a desire to touch.

"...WHAT PROFIT HAVE THE OWNERS EXCEPT TO SEE THEM WITH THEIR EYES?"
ECC 5:11, NKJV

Pornography only gives the viewer a taste of what he is missing. Those salacious images tease a man and then leave him to stew in his own craving. God never designed sex to be a spectator sport. Watching two individuals have sex from the sidelines could never fulfill a person like making love to a real partner. Imagining oneself in the fantasy does not make it so. A magazine or television screen could never give the viewer what he seeks. This is why a guy who watches porn will never have enough. If watching for the first time did not satisfy, know that repeating the behavior won't either.

> "ALL THE LABOR OF MAN IS FOR HIS MOUTH,
> AND YET THE SOUL IS NOT SATISFIED."
> ECC 6:7, NKJV

This inability to touch any of those naked women on the screen is enough to drive any guy crazy. The envy aroused from looking eats away at the viewer and leaves a corrosive wound inside. Before, the man was happy and content with who he was and whatever he was doing. Afterward, the man finds himself unhappy and discontent. All because he is unable to touch that woman on the screen. Looking at pornography has ruined his emotional state. At the end of the day, the voyeur is left feeling empty and hollow inside. His inner world is forever changed. Any initial itch to look was a mild discomfort compared with this torment. Consuming pornography is not a harmless indulgence.

> "...WHEN DESIRE HAS CONCEIVED, IT GIVES BIRTH TO SIN..."
> JAMES 1:15, NKJV

Anyone who samples porn's pleasures will acquire an insatiable lust. This desire begins to pull at the man's heartstrings. The man's sexual tension begins to elevate. Sexual tension arises from conflicting desires pulling the man in opposite directions. Moral duty pulls a man in one direction and carnal passion pulls him in another. To look at porn is to subject oneself to temptation. The same eye candy that gives the viewer an emotional sugar rush now triggers a spiritual war inside. Whenever a man is not careful about what he looks at or the thoughts he entertains, he is allowing certain sinful desires to take root. Sin can produce all sorts of evil desires in a person. Sinful desires are the cause of a man's own undoing.

> "...YOU SHALT NOT COVET YOUR NEIGHBOR'S
> WIFE..."
> Ex 20:17

The porn viewer will come to covet what he sees; watching those graphic images will arouse his jealousy. A man will not soon forget those images he has seen. He will have to carry them with him wherever he goes. Those images will haunt him for the rest of his life. Their memory will forever remind him of what he lacks. The man will find himself having to fight off these rekindled feelings over and over. To be riddled with sinful desires is to be plagued with this curse. Coveting is the root cause behind every other transgression. A thief steals because he covets. An adulterer lies and cheats because he covets his neighbor's wife. A murderer kills someone because they stand in the way of something coveted. If a man does anything bad, it is because sinful coveting leads him to do it. Coveting is a pathway to the dark side.

"CAN AN ETHIOPIAN CHANGE HIS SKIN OR A LEOPARD IT'S SPOTS? NEITHER CAN YOU DO GOOD WHO ARE ACCUSTOMED TO DOING EVIL."
JER 13:23, NIV

It is a folly to think that one can be a porn lover at heart and never act on such sentiments. A man doesn't act inconsistent with his feelings. He may try to resist his own passions for a time, but this never lasts. Eventually, the current of feelings takes everyone away. For wherever the heart points, there the body will go. A man's every action is driven by his thoughts. His desires direct his every choice. The heart is a roadmap to where a man will eventually go. Everything that has ever occurred within the physical world has originated from this invisible place. If those

34

desires are allowed to grow unchecked, they will eventually manifest themselves in the real world. Whatever is allowed to flourish on the inside always manifests itself.

THE RUB

WHY MASTURBATION CAN'T SATISFY

"...EACH OF YOU SHOULD LEARN TO CONTROL
YOUR OWN BODY IN A WAY THAT IS HOLY AND
HONORABLE."
I THESS 4:4, NKJV

Masturbation usually accompanies porn viewing. This should not surprise anyone. Pornography sets a man's passions on fire and the viewer will want to relieve himself of all those pent-up hormonal stresses. A man on fire needs a physical outlet. He lacks the patience to find and woe a partner. The unbearable sexual tension causes him to seek out a quick fix. Therefore, he decides to take matters into his own hands. To a porn viewer, masturbation is a coping mechanism for dealing with all those pent-up sexual frustrations.

For this reason, masturbation is often regarded as a physical need.

> "FOR OUT OF THE HEART PROCEED...ADULTERIES,
> FORNICATION..."
> MT 15:19, NKJV

Of course, sex always involves more than just the physical. The man who masturbates to porn is doing more than just touching himself. He is fantasizing about someone else in his head. He would have no urge to masturbate unless some impure thoughts were already stewing around in his mind (like the fantasy of making love to some woman). Masturbation is not a form of self-love as some would presuppose; it is better characterized as a type of sex in the spirit. When a man discards those salacious fantasies within his head, the need to masturbate falls flat. Remember, the mind and heart always trigger those physical urges inside. A guy cannot really be turned on without experiencing any of those imaginary figures in his mind. The need to love and be loved always accompanies the need to ejaculate.

> "A GOOD TREE CANNOT BEAR BAD FRUIT,
> NOR CAN A BAD TREE BEAR GOOD FRUIT..."
> MT 7:18, NKJV

Half measures make the masturbation habit a struggle to beat. A man will try to refrain from touching himself but never really get those salacious pornographic images out of his head. Those mental sexual images are what drive a guy crazy and arouse his urge to masturbate. Half measures never work. So long as those pornographic images are allowed to replay within the mind, a man will struggle with overcoming his own masturbation habit. Masturbating to porn is an outward symptom to a much deeper problem. If a man really wants to kick the masturbation habit, he must address those underlying urges.

This means doing more than just turning off the pornographic websites; those images must be removed from one's mind altogether.

"THE WORD OF GOD...IS A DISCERNER OF THE THOUGHTS AND INTENTS OF THE HEART."
HEB 4:12, NKJV

The moral question regarding masturbation becomes self-explanatory and clear when seeing things from a deeper spiritual perspective. Who is the man dreaming about when he does this deed? His heart will determine whether the physical act is right or wrong. If a man is dreaming about a woman who is not his wife, then he is committing adultery with someone in his heart. Coveting and spiritual adultery make masturbation a problem, not the act of touching oneself. An easy way to think of it is like this. If a man should not be having sex with the woman in real life, then he should not be entertaining the idea in his dream life either.

"...MAN LOOKS AT THE OUTWARD APPEARANCE, BUT THE LORD LOOKS AT THE HEART." I SAM 16:7

God does not differentiate between adulterers and those who merely dream about it. To Him, their heart resides in the same place. When God judges, He looks at the heart. Therefore, whether a man does the forbidden deed with someone in real life or just fantasizes about it, the condemnation will always be the same. Know that the coveter will suffer the same eternal fate as the adulterer. It is never enough for a man to reform his outward actions; he must reform his heart as well.

"...FIRST CLEANSE THE INSIDE OF THE CUP AND
DISH, THAT THE OUTSIDE OF THEM MAY BE CLEAN
ALSO."
MT 23:26, NKJV

A man's true feelings about masturbation
should change as his perception of the activity
changes. If masturbation were indeed sufficient
to satisfy a man's physical urges, then a guy
would not need a woman at all to gratify himself-
any hole in the wall would do. He would be able
to make himself content just by getting off. But
here is the rub-masturbation never left any guy
satisfied. Masturbating never stopped him from
pining after the beautiful women he sees around
him. Simply dreaming about a woman and
touching oneself does not appear to cut it. In
fact, masturbation will only make the craving
worse. At some level, every guy knows this deep
down in his heart; he knows this to be true from
experience. Obviously, a man desires something

41

more than just a physical release; his need goes deeper than that.

ADULT ENTERTAINMENT
WHY IT PLUCKS THE HEART STRINGS

"THEREFORE, PLEASE HEAR THIS, YOU AFFLICTED,
AND DRUNK BUT NOT WITH WINE."
ISA 51:21, NKJV

The guy who watches pornography is looking for an emotional experience- something that will pluck his heartstrings. He has come to expect porn will provoke certain feelings inside. In the past, watching has taken him on a unique roller coaster ride of emotion. He will watch with bated breath to see how the scene plays out. The thrills will build as the plot progresses and then it will culminate into some exciting conclusion. A viewer wants to be taken on a joy ride. To him, the emotional experience is the appeal.

"…WE SHOULD NO LONGER BE CHILDREN, TOSSED TO AND FRO, AND CARRIED ABOUT WITH EVERY WIND OF DOCTRINE, BY THE TRICKERY OF MEN, IN THE CUNNING CRAFTINESS OF DECEITFUL PLOTTING."
EPHES 4:14, NKJV

Porn producers know what their audiences want. They also know how to give it to them. The industry has developed a playbook on how to make a successful film. Past bestsellers have been studied in detail to discover the reasons behind their success. Every cinematic element has been broken down, dissected, and analyzed. Each component is given a label and categorized according to the different emotions they illicit. These cinematic elements will be woven together into a winning formula. Screen writers know these conventions must be followed if a new film is to sell. When the film hits all the right buttons, the audience marvels and is left mystified. Understanding these tricks of the trade can provide some real insight into their mind manipulation.

"WE DID NOT FOLLOW CLEVERLY DEVISED TALES..."
II PETER 1:16, NAS

Every filmmaker's toolbox begins with the concept of 'show not tell.' A film's underlying message will never be verbalized in an overt manner. A picture of the theme will always be painted instead. Painting the picture enables an audience to visualize the concept in vivid detail. The graphic imagery livens up the viewer's experience. By painting the picture, an audience can plunge headfirst into the scene. Viewers will forget they are watching pixels on a screen and find themselves peering into a window. This kind of immersive experience teleports the mind straight into the setting. It facilitates a type of spiritual projection into a dream world. Audiences can now picture themselves within the story scene.

> "THEY...HAVE GIVEN THEMSELVES UP TO SENSUALITY..."
> EPHES 4:19, ESV

Producers want their viewers to feel and experience everything important in the film for themselves. Mere assertions can feel contrived and might raise a viewer's skepticism. Just telling someone about an emotion will hold less of an impact than allowing an audience to feel it for themselves. The emotional messaging will never be stated outright; it is always embedded straight into the scene for audiences to discover. Presenting the underlying theme in storyboard form enables visualization. Seeing the message for oneself will turn them into believers.

"COME BACK TO YOUR SENSES AS YOU OUGHT..."
I COR 15:34, NIV

Audiences love this. Awakening a viewer's senses make the experience feel more real. In real life, emotions almost never get communicated in a direct fashion. Audiences can pick up on the most subtle of signals. They will be able to find the answer using their own faculties. Less information and more vivid detail provides the story depth and will keep the experience primal. Audiences want to feel those emotions within their gut. Everyone wants a personal experience on the feeling wavelength.

"TAKE CAREFUL HEED TO YOURSELVES...LEST YOU
ACT CORRUPTLY AND MAKE FOR YOURSELVES A
CARVED IMAGE IN THE FORM OF ANY FIGURE:
THE LIKENESS OF MALE OR FEMALE."
DT 4:16, NKJV

In this imaginary world, audiences will start looking for a character they can relate with. Great care is taken in casting a woman for these scenes. Writers will put a lot of effort into breathing life into her character. Animating her personality will humanize her and make her relatable. Everything in her body language, tone of voice, facial expressions, and pace of movement will all be carefully choreographed so that the character embodies all the right emotions. A filmmaker knows an audience will find themselves drawn to such likeable figures. They will sympathize with a relatable character. A female figure who embodies the same desires will cause a viewer to emotionally engage with her.

"YOU SHALL BURN THE CARVED IMAGES
...LEST YOU BE SNARED BY IT."
DT 7:25, NKJV

Film producers know a specific viewing demographic can be targeted just by creating the right female character as bait. The more universal her appeal is, the broader the viewing audience will be. When done right, viewers will become so enamored with this female character that their emotional states link. At this point, the audience will begin to see everything through the lens of this main character. Viewers will identify with characters they love. An audience will want to see what happens to their beloved character in the end. Do they achieve their desired goals? Does the plot unfold in some fabulous and interesting way? To find out viewers will buckle up for the ride and go on the adventure.

> "...BY YOUR MAGIC SPELL
> ALL THE NATIONS WERE LED ASTRAY."
> REV 18:23, NIV

The entire goal behind making these relatable characters was to get an audience to emotionally engage and follow along on the journey. The desire to live out some vicarious experience with these imaginary characters turns the viewer into an emotional pawn. In the hands of a capable storyteller, that imaginary character will now serve as an emotional voodoo doll for the viewer. Whatever happens to the main character in the story will now impact the viewer emotionally. His outlook being manipulated by the emotional connection he has with that imaginary character.

"...ALL THE PEOPLE HUNG ON HIS WORDS."
LUKE 19:48, NIV

The storyline becomes an elaborate plot devised to manipulate the viewer's emotions. Everything in the scene will be structured to lead the audience down a given direction. Clothing, props, and décor are all carefully chosen to set the ambiance in the room. The filmmaker will try to influence a viewer's thoughts by manipulating the point of view. The camera focus will make certain features stand out. Sudden close ups will accentuate specific details. Even the background music will be carefully chosen to guide the viewer on how to feel about what is perceived. The one writing the script is controlling this narrative.

"AND THOSE WHO MAKE IDOLS ARE JUST LIKE
THEM, AS ARE ALL WHO TRUST IN THEM."
PS 115:8, NLT

To the viewer, a popular storyline will become more than just an inner amusement that preoccupies the mind for a while. Those popular scenes will be remembered; audiences will replay and rehearse those same favorite scenes back within their own head. A viewer will want to relive these experiences. Everyone is looking for ways to achieve their own happily ever after. A popular plot that titillates the senses will give a man ideas on how to accomplish this. The strategy will come to be enshrined as a roadmap for living. People are known to try and reenact those popular story lines in the real world; life does begin to imitate art.

THE CLIMAX

UNDERSTANDING PORN'S HOOK

"...I DID NOT WITHOLD MY HEART FROM ANY
PLEASURE."
Ecc 2:10, NKJV

What exactly does a guy get out of viewing
pornography? Embedded within every porn film
is the climax of the story. Every porn film
promises some type of climax. Foreshadowing
tells the audience where the story is leading. A
steady progression of titillating details heighten
the viewer's expectations. The anticipation of the
climax is what keeps the viewer tuned in. The
climax generates the emotional high people want.
This cinematic element is named for the
emotional effect it has on audiences. It also

happens to be what makes pornography so addictive. Audiences are looking for this emotional payoff.

> "...BEHOLD, HE STANDS BEHIND OUR WALL;
> HE IS LOOKING THROUGH THE WINDOWS,
> GAZING THROUGH THE LATTICE."
> SONGS 2:9, NKJV

Audiences know a porn star will show them everything they want to see; they are looking forward to more than just the woman shedding her clothes. Viewers want to see the woman in action; they know a porn star won't hold back her feelings. She makes noise about it. Her physical responses to the man's touch, the tremors reverberating through her body, the expressions on her face, the way she looks at him, and all her guttural groanings tell a man she likes it; they tell a man she likes him. On screen, a porn actress loves sex. She doesn't just profess her desire; she shows it in explicit ways. Everything in her body

54

language, her actions, and her words emanates this passion. A porn star will go to great lengths to show her enthusiasm for sex on the screen. Not only does she give herself over to the man for his pleasure, but she brands herself with tattoos to emphasize the statement. A porn star embodies the kind of passion a man wants from a woman in the bedroom.

"WHAT A PERSON DESIRES IS UNFAILING LOVE."
PROV 19:22, NIV

This kind of female sexual passion grabs a guy by his heart strings. A guy derives immense pleasure from seeing it. Before he even notices it, his heart will start racing and his emotions begin to soar. These magical feelings have a powerful drug-like effect on a guy. The rush of chemical endorphins trigger an emotional contagion. Why does a guy enjoy seeing a woman swoon with pleasure so much? Why do these theatrics play with his head? The viewer believes he has found love. His heart bonds with the figure on the screen. The same dynamic intended to knit a husband and wife emotionally together is what binds the viewer's heart to the screen. The man is witnessing what he has wanted all his life- a woman who will exhibit sexual submission with heart. When a guy witnesses this kind of behavior in a woman, his heart pops out of his chest.

"COME, LET US TAKE OUR FILL OF LOVE UNTIL MORNING,
LET US DELIGHT OURSELVES WITH LOVE."
PROV 7:18, NKJV

God's command to every wife is the magic formula for winning over the male heart. The porn star adorns herself in the eyes of her male audience by exhibiting this enthusiastic submission. Submission with heart is a very precious thing in the sight of a man. The porn star can establish an emotional connection with her male audience because she exhibits this kind of passion on screen. Her sexual passion makes her dream like. She rises to stardom because submission with heart underlies her every word and action. Dream girls come in many shapes, colors, and sizes, but every one of them possess this common trait.

> "BEFORE I WAS EVEN AWARE, MY SOUL HAD MADE ME AS THE CHARIOTS OF MY NOBLE PEOPLE."
> SONGS 6:12, NKJV

It should not surprise anyone that a guy might interpret a woman's sexual passion as love. To a guy, real romance involves sex. A guy is more in touch with his own sexual desires than with his emotions. He knows sex is dear to his heart. He associates his own heart with his hormones. For a guy, these two things are often lumped together. A guy will often think he loves a woman because he is sexually attracted to her. Therefore, men interpret a woman's sexual attraction as love.

> "HOW FAIR AND HOW PLEASANT YOU ARE,
> O LOVE, WITH YOUR DELIGHTS."
> SONGS 7:6, NKJV

Nothing is more pleasurable to the male viewer than to witness a porn star climax. To a man, a woman's sexual climax is tangible proof she enjoyed the experience. Nothing affirms a guy's manhood more than to witness a woman have this sexual pleasure. God never intended sex to be enjoyed exclusively for men; He intended women to enjoy the event also. Therefore, God has made satisfying a woman in bed a man's ultimate satisfaction. Men have been given the burden of ensuring their female partners enjoy sex. A man's self-worth is tied to his sexual performance. A guy will always feel like less of a man until he can pleasure a woman in this way.

Deep down a man wants a woman's respect. Respect is a kind of love for what one can do and nothing commands that respect more than getting a female partner to climax. The task may not be easy, but the challenge makes the feat glorious. A guy will watch porn to get a taste of this affirmation. The feelings of sexual validation are the emotional payoff.

> "LET [YOUR WIFE'S] BREASTS SATISFY YOU AT ALL TIMES, AND ALWAYS BE ENRAPTURED WITH HER LOVE. FOR WHY SHOULD YOU, MY SON, BE ENRAPTURED BY AN IMMORAL WOMAN, AND BE EMBRACED IN THE ARMS OF A SEDUCTRESS?"
> PROV 5:19-20

Female nudity may draw the male eye to porn, but it is female passion that ensnares it. A guy can always walk away from a woman's outward beauty, but a woman's love is much harder to get away from. A porn viewer will come to idolize those sirens on the screen for their ability to stir

59

such magical feelings inside. It will be a struggle to stop looking at them. For a guy, to look is to feel. If a guy is deprived of looking than he is also deprived of feeling those wonderful sensations. A guy may not be in touch with his own feelings, but this does not imply he lacks them. He may not understand every subtle que, but he will certainly feel the overall effect in his heart. Behind the addictive urge to watch is a real need to feel loved.

THE WET DREAM

WHY IT RINGS HOLLOW

"EVERYTHING THEY DO IS DONE FOR PEOPLE TO
SEE..."
MT 23:5, NIV

The adult film industry puts on an aggressive
marketing campaign to glamorize the porn star's
lifestyle. At their conventions, porn stars will be
showcased around as beautiful people living
fulfilling lives. Porn stars will go around bragging
about how much they enjoy their profession and
lead people to think that they get paid a lot of
money to do it. This peddled narrative leaves a
strong impression with the spectator; it leads
them to think that being a porn star is some great
thing. The act certainly plays on hearts. For every

year, thousands of men and women will flock to the porn industry for employment. Hoping to live out this wet dream.

"THEN I LOOKED ON ALL THE WORKS THAT MY HANDS HAD DONE...AND INDEED ALL WAS VANITY..."
ECC 2:11A, NKJV

But reality is not like the movies. Audiences don't appreciate the ordeal every porn star must go through to entertain them. Those newbies trying to get into the industry don't know what they are in for. They have yet to experience what happens on the other side of the camera. It would be wise for a person to do their due diligence before venturing into such a profession. Nobody needs to learn these painful lessons the hard way. Plenty of testimonials have been written on the subject by actors and actresses who have played these roles already. The Porn star Belladonna once said "I had to do a lot of things I couldn't imagine anyone wanting to do." (Dorough, 2011) A summarized description of these experiences goes something like this:

"THEREFORE, I HATED LIFE BECAUSE THE WORK THAT WAS DONE UNDER THE SUN WAS DISTRESSING TO ME..."
ECC 2:17, NKJV

Screen sex is not as glamorous as everyone thinks. Screen sex is performing for the camera; it is not real sex. Those sexual acts done in front of the camera are performed for the amusement of the paying audience not the enjoyment of the actors. None of these acts are spontaneous. Every scene is planned, coordinated, and mapped out in gory detail. Just shooting a pornographic sex scene is hard work. The unnatural positions required to accommodate both the equipment and crew make the work uncomfortable and physically taxing. Having to do multiple shots from different angles will make the effort tedious and grueling. Most full-length productions are made within just a few days. Costars are expected to work from early morning until late at night. The long hours can be exhausting. One could say the pressure to perform strips all the fun out of the activity.

> "I WILL LIFT YOUR SKIRTS OVER YOUR FACE, I WILL SHOW THE NATIONS YOUR NAKEDNESS, AND THE KINGDOMS YOUR SHAME..."
> NAHUM 3:5, NKJV

An audience doesn't appreciate the ordeal every performer must go thru to do a sex scene. For to be completely naked in front of a camera is to feel vulnerable. A high-definition camera gets shoved between a performer's legs to take close ups in full lighting. It will magnify every defect- every pimple, varicose vein, stretch mark, or cottage cheese layer of fat. A performer must always worry about whether they wiped their rear end good enough. For to think anyone might see some unflattering feature would make them a laughingstock. It should not be surprising then that a performer might be overly concerned with how their private parts look. Screen sex makes every performer feel downright self-conscious.

To work as a porn star is to feel more vulnerable than anything else.

"I WILL CAST ABOMINABLE FILTH UPON YOU, MAKE YOU VILE, AND MAKE YOU A SPECTACLE."
NAHUM 3:6, NKJV

Filming a sex scene can be quite the traumatic experience. For every sexual act must be performed in public. Behind that camera stands an entire support crew that watches and analyzes the event from every angle. The porn star will face a gauntlet of scrutiny from them for every bounce, flop, or accidental fart caught on camera. Even the male costar feels a tremendous amount of pressure to perform. For everyone must wait

65

on him to get and keep his erection. If he ejaculates too early and the crew misses it, the scene will have to be redone. The entire crew will have to work longer because of it. Don't think a male performer won't be ridiculed for this. Women will be criticized for the size of their boobs and be told to get implants. Over the course of making these films, performers will be criticized for both their physical appearance and their sexual performance. These criticisms will make the work more distressing than enjoyable. A newbie doesn't realize they will have to cope with all this criticism going thru it. Before it is over, the performer will incur a great deal of emotional trauma.

"IT SHALL COME TO PASS THAT ALL WHO LOOK
UPON YOU WILL FLEE FROM YOU..."
NAHUM 3:7A, NKJV

Of course, the trauma doesn't stop when the lights and cameras are turned off. The social price a performer pays for capturing any of these perverted moments on film is enormous. Viewers will never think of them again in the same way. The porn star will forever be labeled as some kind of sex crazed maniac. The performer will never be able to live this label down. Whenever she is recognized in public, she will be stared at and shunned. Fans who would look on her nakedness in private don't want to be associated with her in public. They distance themselves from "those kinds of people." One Insider said people entering this profession become "sociologically damned forever." (Dorough, 2011)

"WOUNDS AND DISHONOR HE WILL GET, AND HIS
REPROACH WILL NOT BE WIPED AWAY."
PROV 6:33, NKJV

Pornographic footage becomes a permanent record for all to see. This footage will often find its way on to public websites that make the content available for free. Therefore, anybody can look at those embarrassing moments at any time. In most cases, a performer will not own the rights to their own pornographic content and they will have no control over who looks at it. Those embarrassing sex scenes will forever tarnish a person's reputation. Performers will have to explain themselves to all their family and friends. It must be especially hard to explain those shameful scenes to one's parents and children. No matter what the porn star goes on to do, he or she will always find themselves having to explain themselves. Some experiences can't be taken back. The terrible social stigma follows the porn star everywhere they go.

"...WHERE SHALL I SEEK COMFORTERS FOR YOU?"
NAHUM 3:7B, NKJV

A porn star will not be able to go home to someone who will sympathize with their plight. Most of the people working in this industry have had to kiss their love life goodbye. The average person does not want to be in a romantic relationship with someone who has sex with other people. For some, dating a porn star might seem like a novelty, but this shine does wears off. Normal jealousy makes seeing a partner work in the profession a real struggle and those who continue to perform will only create for themselves a lot of relational drama. This happens even to performers who are dating other people in the industry. Nobody can endure this kind of arrangement for too long. Eventually, the career wrecks the relationship. Because of these problems, a lot of porn stars just stop dating altogether. Hidden behind the glamor are individuals suffering a lonely miserable existence.

"...THERE WAS NO PROFIT UNDER THE SUN."
ECC 2:11B, NKJV

The money is never worth it. The total compensation a performer receives for taking on this trouble is not much higher than what the average blue-collar worker might receive. (Dorough, 2011) Porn work does not pay any lasting benefits; the job is contractual and unsteady. Porn contracts are written to protect the industry not the performer. The higher ups will rake in all the profits and the worker will assume all the risks (and there are plenty of risks to assume). A newcomer who is not trained as a lawyer and is eager to break into the industry will unknowingly sign away all their rights. Newbies will get taken for suckers. A performer shouldn't think an agent or a manager in the adult entertainment industry would ever have their best interests at heart. These nefarious individuals have a vested interest in siphoning away the performer's personal earnings. The industry doesn't want the public to be aware of these harsh realities. Otherwise, people might not be so eager to sign up.

"...LET THEIR TABLE BECOME A SNARE AND A
TRAP..."
ROM 11:9, NKJV

Once a person starts working in this industry, it will become a struggle to get out. Pornographic footage blacklists a person from a lot of other employment opportunities. The average company will not want to be associated with a porn star; the social stigma is bad for business. A porn star who wants to move past this kind of work may find themselves stuck.

71

Most porn stars live alone and broke because the industry destroyed both their personal and professional life. When all the money and other prospects dry up, these same actors come crawling back to the industry for subsistence.

> "YOU BUILT YOUR HIGH PLACES AT THE HEAD OF EVERY ROAD, AND MADE YOUR BEAUTY TO BE ABHORRED. YOU OFFERED YOURSELF TO EVERYONE WHO PASSED BY, AND MULTIPLIED YOUR ACTS OF HARLOTRY."
> EZEK 16:25, NKJV

Of course, to stay on this career track only gets progressively worse for the performer. Understand a woman degrades herself doing porn. Showing one's skin to the masses removes all the mystery. As a woman provides more visual content for her audience, their fascination with seeing her naked body fades and she will become less valuable to them. In time, every new toy loses it's luster. Demand goes down with supply. If a woman wants to keep up everyone's interest, she must continue to do more and more outlandish things. The industry is always looking for individuals who are willing to reenact more visually shocking, gross, painful, and outright dangerous things. The industry pays a premium for ever-increasing debauched behavior. The only way to get ahead in this industry is the willingness to go down.

"FOR THUS SAYS THE LORD GOD: SURELY I WILL DELIVER YOU INTO THE HAND OF THOSE YOU HATE..."
EZEK 23:28, NKJV

If a woman wants to continue working in this field, she must be prepared to endure greater levels of degradation. Normal sex is just the tip of the iceberg. The industry is always pushing the boundaries of what is safe. The porn star will be pressured to reenact things that will take a toll on her physical body and may even put her in the hospital. How low is a person willing to stoop for money? What kind of sick things are they prepared to endure? The outsider would be surprised at what the lure of money might get a person to do. Individuals desperate for money are prepared to do desperate things. It's hard to say no to someone signing the paycheck or offering that first career break. The process itself breaks down a person's will to resist.

THEY WILL DEAL HATEFULLY WITH YOU,
TAKE AWAY ALL YOU HAVE WORKED FOR,
AND LEAVE YOU NAKED AND BARE."
EZEK 23:29, NKJV

Employers know this and use it to get people to do things they would not normally feel comfortable doing. A lot of coercion and exploitation goes on in the industry. Many games are played to convince young girls that giving out free sexual favors is part of the scope of work. (Jameson, 2010) [10] Sometimes, no pretext must be given to get a person to create a scene. At 18, a young adult doesn't know what they can refuse. The industry preys upon abused people who have no sense of boundaries. These individuals will be run through the proverbial meat grinder. If an actor under contract expresses any reservations about doing a particular sex scene, the corporate bosses will just pressure and coerce them into getting the project done. The threat of being fired is an effective tool for coercion. In some cases, individuals are even forced against their will. A lot of sex trafficking goes on to make some of these films. A viewer cannot always tell if the porn he is watching is consensual or not. Executives in the industry don't care about these individuals; they only care about the money. The industry will chew these individuals up and spit them out. To an executive, porn stars have been known to be referred to as "throw away people." (Dorough, 2011)[9]

"YOU WILL BE FILLED WITH DRUNKENNESS AND
SORROW,
THE CUP OF HORROR AND DESOLATION..."
EZEK 23:33, NKJV

Working in the adult film industry is dangerous to one's spiritual, emotional, and physical well-being. Most cannot handle this kind of work for very long. The average timeframe a girl will spend in the profession is two to three years at most. Everyone hits their limits. Either the actress hits her limit of what she is willing to act out or fans stop watching her in total disgust over what she has done. Being a spectacle is not the kind of attention a woman wants to gain for herself. The degrading acts will permanently scar a person. Performers do their best to survive these degrading moments given the contractual pressures. Many will consume drugs just to get through it. In the wake of these experiences, several have reported developing suicidal tendencies. The occupation of a porn star is not something to be envied.

> "...YOU SHALL BREAK IT'S SHARDS,
> AND TEAR AT YOUR OWN BREASTS;
> FOR I HAVE SPOKEN, SAYS THE LORD GOD."
> EZEK 23:34, NKJV

A performer does not enjoy their work as much as an outsider might think. If the truth be told, most porn stars hate their work and hate themselves for doing it. If a viewer really knew how much pain and abuse these performers suffered, one might find it a turn-off and stop consuming the product. The porn industry cannot afford to let this to happen. Emotions will get feigned for the cameras. Insiders describe it as "going through the motions without the emotions." (Paul, 2006) [8] Actors and actresses know impressing an audience is their job. An audience would not enjoy the scene if it looked like the costars did not. Performers play it up to get paid.

Those feelings between co-stars are not what they appear on screen. The viewer is envious of an affection that is not there. This is why the whole porn industry rings hollow. Everything produced by the porn industry is a fiction; it does not resemble real life. In short, the industry is selling a fantasy.

SUSPENSION OF DISBELIEF
NO POPPING THE EMOTIONAL BUBBLE

"LET US NOT SLEEP, AS OTHERS DO, BUT LET US
WATCH AND BE SOBER."
I THESS 5:6, NKJV

Of course, learning these facts about the industry
do not always deter viewers from sliding down
the rabbit hole. Some people don't enjoy their
reality and want that mental escape to porn. The
images projected on the screen may be an
illusion, but those euphoric sensations still feel
palpable. A viewer still knows the fantasy brings
him pleasure whether the narrative is verified or
not. Sometimes this is the only thing that matters.
For these individuals, a state of drunkenness is
more preferrable than being sober.

"THEY WILL REJECT THE TRUTH,
AND CHASE AFTER MYTHS."
II TIM 4:4, NLT

Suspension of disbelief will allow a man to forget those images are not real. Anyone who has ever forgotten they were sitting in a movie theatre during a film has experienced suspension of disbelief. A man can still dream about a woman he likes if he is not able to acquire her in real life. In the world of fantasy, a person can have access to just about anyone and do anything with them their heart desires. The world of fantasy can become a person's escape from the boredom and emptiness of real life. Buying into the story arc is the only thing needed to live out the fantasy and enjoy the pleasure.

"...THEY PERISH BECAUSE THEY REFUSED TO LOVE
THE TRUTH AND SO BE SAVED."
II THESS 2:10, NIV

Many porn viewers don't want their emotional bubble popped. An individual must remain asleep to enjoy the dream. Turning on one's critical thinking skills might awaken them from their half-conscious state. A person enjoying the dream does not want this to happen. The fear that reality might kill their enjoyment creates an aversion to knowing the truth. As a result, these individuals will willingly tune out the information. The dreamer doesn't want to be confused by facts. This desire for porn's pleasure creates an underlying need to self-deceive.

"WATCH OUT! DON'T LET YOUR HEARTS BE
DULLED BY CAROUSING AND DRUNKENNESS, AND BY
THE WORRIES OF THIS LIFE. DON'T LET THAT DAY
CATCH YOU UNAWARE."
LUKE 21:34, NLT

Of course, a lot of people don't see anything wrong with living in a fantasy world. At first glance, indulging in a fantasy doesn't seem to impose any real consequences. In a dream world, nobody fears getting pregnant or contracting a venereal disease. An outsider may find someone who talks to their sex doll as strange, but most would see the activity as innocent. The culture encourages people to fantasize and masturbate. These activities are seen as ways for people to get in touch with their own sexuality. People are emboldened to let down their guard. To zone everything else out and focus on the screen. Pornographic films are seen as a safe place. This world of fantasy is thought to be a domain where deviant emotions can be indulged in without any fear of reprisal. For this reason, the medium will be used as a vicarious outlet; a place to live out outlandish things a person might be otherwise too afraid to express in the real world. A viewer believes whatever happens there will stay there.

"KEEP YOUR HEART WITH ALL DILIGENCE,
FOR OUT OF IT SPRINGS THE ISSUES OF LIFE."
PROV 4:23

But nobody ever thinks about the risks involved in exposing one's heart to these things. Protecting the heart is never thought of as a necessary measure for one's own personal safety. Remember, whatever captivates the heart takes the whole person into bondage. The body will always follow the heart wherever it goes- even unto death. Wherever the heart goes, there the rest of a person must always follow. Physical restraint cannot contain the heart's madness. For everyone enchanted by the song will answer the siren's call. When the opportunity to jump ship presents itself, know those enamored individuals will always take it.

"...FOR BY YOUR SORCERY
ALL THE NATIONS WERE DECEIVED."
REV 18:23, NKJV

Losing touch with reality does have consequences. The trance of entertainment will impair a viewer's personal judgement. Zoning out turns a person into a zombie. An individual in this catatonic state will become hyper suggestible. His mind will be closed but his heart will be open. Allowing oneself to be swept up in all the emotion will make someone vulnerable to exploitation. A viewer won't notice whatever a filmmaker tries to implant within his own head. His conscious brain won't notice any of the signals, but his subconscious will certainly pick them up. The subconscious can pick up on the smallest of nuances. As a result, the observer will begin to feel things but not be able to wrap their mind around as to why. Porn's maddening wine will prevent a person from thinking straight. Nothing seems wrong when it has been made to feel right.

"I SLEEP, BUT MY HEART IS AWAKE..."
SONGS 5:2, NKJV

Producers and marketers love to employ subliminal signals as a kind of subtext in their films. These devices allow them to form a favorable impression about a product just by leaving the faintest impression with an audience. The associations made may be poor at face value, but an enchanted audience won't be able to recognize it. A viewer will feel a need to have the product and will not understand why. Feelings can be more persuasive than logic. Producers know speaking straight to the heart like this will create a very loyal customer base. Playing with a viewer's emotions is the strongest form of manipulation. Nobody can deny these tactics influence a viewer's thoughts and buying habits. Advertisers would not invest billions in marketing if it did not.

> "...THE SEED SHOULD SPROUT AND GROW,
> HE HIMSELF DOES NOT KNOW HOW."
> MRK 4:27, NKJV

The belief that pornographic fantasies hold no consequences is only true until it changes a person. Don't think that whatever gets implanted within the heart won't eventually manifest itself into the real world. For whatever is implanted and nurtured will always materialize. For whatever a man glorifies in, that he becomes. Pornographic films serve as a spiritual training ground. A training ground for dark feelings to be cultivated within the heart. As Wes Craven would say, film serves as "a boot camp for their psyche." [23] Pornography changes people for the worse. For once a man begins to glorify in things that are bad, he will no longer be civilized.

PORNOGRAPHIC INTOXICATION
A DEMONIC ENCHANTMENT

"...THE THINGS WHICH THE GENTILES SACRIFICE,
THEY SACRIFICE TO DEMONS."
I COR 10:20, NKJV

A viewer who is enamored with the pleasures of porn does not really understand what he is chasing. The pornographic high has nothing to do with actual people. In fact, plenty of viewers abandon their real-life partner in favor of pursuing porn. Pornography is responsible for the "man drought" seen around the world; it kills a man's desire to have sex with real women. Many porn addicts have come to believe a real partner gets in the way of the fantasy and disrupts the high. In truth, the porn addict is looking for an endorphin rush and not a particular person.

"... THE SPIRIT OF HARLOTRY HAS CAUSED THEM TO STRAY..."
HOSEA 4:12, NKJV

He is hypnotized by the images flashing across the screen. The charms of the porn star seduce him into a dream-like state. The man loses himself getting caught up with the pornographic storyline. He wants to be taken on a magic carpet ride. By allowing the dream to descend and enter the body, the viewer can tap into that emotional enchantment he craves. His pleasure comes alive as reality slips away. His spirit will become one with the female character seen on the screen. His feelings move in unison to her every action and reaction. In truth, porn viewing is a type of spiritual seance. The viewer resembles a shaman entering a trance. He becomes hyper-suggestible to every underlying theme presented to him on the screen. Suspension of disbelief opens the door into this altered spiritual state.

"Ephraim is Joined to Idols..."
Hosea 4:17

The viewer may imagine himself making love to the woman on the screen. He may also think the woman is making love to him in return. In truth, he is having sex with the images in his head. What the guy encounters in his mind's eye may appear to have a human form, but this manifestation is far from human. In a literal sense, the woman of his dreams is an apparition; the entity he is copulating with is a noncorporeal being.

"...THE SACRIFICE OF PAGANS ARE OFFERED TO
DEMONS, NOT TO GOD, AND I DO NOT WANT YOU TO
BE PARTICIPANT WITH DEMONS."
I COR 10:20, NIV

The porn user doesn't really understand what he is in a love affair with. The wet dream he indulges in is nothing more than an animistic ritual; a spiritual ceremony in which he communes with demonic spirits. The pleasurable sensations the dreamer feels in these "love" sessions is fueled by the specter. The phantom enters the mind and gives the body chills. As a result, many will even scream out the name 'god' being intimate with it. Behind every one of those forbidden mental images lies a demon. The physical medium used to get in contact with these entities is immaterial. Demonic spirits can inhabit just about anything. The pornographic intoxication a man is really seeking after is a demonic enchantment.

PORNOGRAPHIC INTOXICATION

> "...IF YOU HAVE BITTER ENVY AND SELF-SEEKING IN YOUR HEARTS...THIS WISDOM DOES NOT DESCEND FROM ABOVE, BUT IS EARTHLY, SENSUAL, DEMONIC."
> JAMES 3:14-15, NKJV

In the ancient world, pagans knew they were communing with spirits when they did this. Their religious practices often incorporated sexual activity into their idol worship. The high places upon which these sexual fertility rites would be practiced were the equivalent of a public stage where everyone could see them. Such pornographic exhibitions were sure to draw onlookers and stir excitement among the crowds. It caused everyone around to want to join the action. The ancient peoples would frequent temples and pay tribute to their overseers just for the chance at hiring one of their priestesses as a ritual harlot. A man would take this woman into some dark smoke-filled room and use her sexually to commune with his 'god.'

The patrons would attribute those pleasurable feelings they experienced to the false gods they worshipped. Their hearts were taken captive by these pagan rituals. The widespread use of these practices led to their civilization's demise.

> "YOUR PEOPLE WHOM YOU BROUGHT OUT OF EGYPT HAVE ACTED CORRUPTLY...THEY HAVE MADE THEMSELVES A MOLDED IMAGE."
> DT 9:12, NKJV

The viewer does not realize the kind of forces he is unleashing by watching porn. The modern age has forgotten what these practices do to an individual or society at large. The pagan rituals of a bygone era have long since passed; their ancient relics only fill museums now. As a result, the harm these practices have caused have faded from memory. Proper measures are not being taken to keep these practices buried. Making anything into an idol holds severe consequences for both the individual and society at large. An idol becomes the highest priority in a person's life. This new spiritual pecking order causes everything else to take a back seat- even moral boundaries and common decency. An idolater won't let anything get in the way of obtaining his emotional fix. He depends upon his idol just to be happy. He must have his precious love at all costs. If this means stepping over someone, it will be done. For nothing can take precedence over a 'god' in one's life. For this reason, idols corrupt an individual. "Doing the loving thing" no longer sets the agenda. This is why a porn addiction will always be characterized as a vice.

ADDICTION PSYCHOLOGY
WHY THEY DON'T HAVE IT IN THEM TO STOP

"WHERE DO WARS AND FIGHTS COME FROM
AMONG YOU? DO THEY NOT COME FROM YOUR
DESIRES FOR PLEASURE THAT WAR IN YOUR
MEMBERS?"
JAMES 4:1, NKJV

A man addicted to porn is haunted by the
pornographic images he has seen. The siren's
voices call to him. Those imaginary figures visit
him in his dreams and ask for him by name; they
have a way of showing up at the most
inconvenient of times. It is hard to concentrate
on anything else when those mental images are
always trying to creep back in and take over. The
mental fog impairs a man's ability to focus. These

dark sexual thoughts become an unwelcome companion.

> "...ABSTAIN FROM FLESHLY LUSTS WHICH WAR AGAINST THE SOUL."
> I PETER 2:11 NKJV

An addict will recognize this struggle within his own members. He can feel that compulsive need to look. He knows something inside is always trying to pull him back to porn. He understands these urges are warring within his soul. The struggle with a porn addiction is really a spiritual battle of the heart. Therefore, a man will need spiritual insight to overcome it.

> "...FIRST CLEANSE THE INSIDE OF THE CUP AND DISH, THAT THE OUTSIDE OF THEM MAY BE CLEAN ALSO."
> MT 23: 26, NKJV

An individual will often draw a blank on how to shake these feelings. He may try to seek out some professional help to beat the addiction.

But medicine and psychology cannot help much in this area. For these scientific disciplines remain hesitant to delve into the spiritual dimension. Therefore, their conclusions and prescriptions can only go so far. The same could be said about a lot of religious sources of help. Religion also doesn't want to dig into the world of feelings and emotions. When it comes to sexual desires, religious practitioners prefer to only scratch the surface. Therefore, their doctrines and dogmas could never address the root cause. To properly address a porn addiction, one must look at things at the desire level. Those sinful feelings working beneath the surface must be seen and understood for what they are.

"Sin, taking opportunity of the commandment, produced in me all manner of evil desire..."
Rom 7:8, NKJV

Sinful desires have a will of their own. It is as if these urges can recognize moments of opportunity. Whenever a certain stimulus is anticipated, the brain releases certain chemical neurotransmitters triggering a person to look. Creating that itch which nags to be scratched. Sin is always seeking to subjugate a man and goad him into looking. It won't let a man rest until he complies. If an individual does not comply with any of these internal demands, the body will begin to undergo withdrawals. Going without now make the individual feel bad. These painful withdrawals are what make it hard to stop.

"DO YOU NOT KNOW THAT TO WHOM YOU
PRESENT YOURSELVES SLAVES TO OBEY,
YOU ARE THAT ONE'S SLAVE WHOM YOU OBEY..."
ROM 6:16 NKJV

A man may want to change but he cannot
bring himself to do it. This persistent pestering
takes a toll on his person; it leads him to believe
that the only way to find relief is to succumb. He
fears the inward pain of letting go. He is afraid
his body might go into convulsions if he attempts
to detox. He thinks this pain of letting go will
drive him insane and this fear makes him resistant
to any kind of change. In truth, the man is afraid
of a spiritual crash.

"...THE UNFAITHFUL ARE TRAPPED BY EVIL
DESIRES."
PROV 11:6, NIV

Therefore, an addict holds fast to his desire
and allows it to set his course. His behavior cycle
repeats itself because he does not know how to

make it without his drug. The fear of letting go is overpowering his desire to break free. He might even become hostile to anyone who suggests it. These overpowering sensations can make an addict feel trapped. What he wills, he can no longer practice. The inability to exercise any sort of restraint shows a man has lost control.

> "IF, THEN, I DO WHAT I WILL NOT TO DO…
> IT IS NO LONGER I WHO DO IT,
> BUT SIN THAT DWELLS IN ME."
> ROM 7:16-17, NKJV

This condition should bring a guy to an unsettling revelation. If a man is not in control of what he does, then someone else is. If He is not steering the car himself, then another entity has the wheel. Something else within his own members is controlling what he does. Something else that is not good. Whenever a man chooses to consume porn, he is partaking in a Faustian bargain- a deal with the Devil. The trade is always pleasure in exchange for possession.

> "SATAN ROSE UP AGAINST ISRAEL AND INCITED DAVID
> TO TAKE A CENSUS OF ISRAEL."
> I CHRON 21:1, NIV

Satan is always trying to manipulate a man by his desires. He calls upon his subjects to serve him by tugging at their heartstrings. He is beckoning them to follow him by seducing them away like the pied piper. An addicted person will sense this calling and begin to yearn. He will long for the dream to enter in and flood his soul once again. For a few brief moments, he hopes those fleeting passions will enliven him. In deriving pleasure from these things, a man is making himself one with these demonic spirits. His own life force is bound to these ethereal beings.

> "...HE ENLARGES HIS DESIRE AS HELL,
> AND HE IS LIKE DEATH, AND CANNOT BE
> SATISFIED..."
> HAB 2:5, NKJV

Of course, the man who does this would be chasing a fleeting pleasure. For demons never give away the carrot they use to entice people. Otherwise, their enchanted subjects would stop moving. Satan must keep a person hungry to fulfill his will; so he keeps a man chasing in order to string him along. Anyone who chases these phantoms will be kept in a perpetual state of want. The person will come to bemoan this deplorable choice; he will live a miserable existence.

> "THOSE WHO REGARD WORTHLESS IDOLS,
> FORSAKE THEIR OWN MERCY."
> JONAH 2:8, NKJV

The man who derives pleasure from the cup of demons will find himself accursed. For to give in to these sinful urges is to become Satan's instrument. The devil only uses his subjects as sacrificial pawns. He drives them to do something foolish for some nefarious reason. Satan will run his subjects off the cliff in serving his purpose; death is always the eventual outcome. Understand if a man begins to slip, he may not be able to stop himself. He may fall farther and faster than he ever intended. Those who cling to their own sinful affections forsake their own redemption.

"...THEY WILL COME TO THEIR SENSES
AND ESCAPE THE TRAP OF THE DEVIL,
WHO HAS TAKEN THEM CAPTIVE TO DO HIS WILL."
II TIM 2:26, NIV

This tragedy happens because an addict is reluctant to fight his own demons. What will the man's life be like when the demonic entity leaves his body? An addict can't see past the death of his desire; he doesn't see any hope in severing this tie. To an addict, giving up on porn's pleasure is equated with dying to self. There are many types of death; all of them can be characterized as some kind of separation of spirit from the body. The truth is nobody ever truly dies letting go of pornography. Life always goes on and people learn to thrive without it. That shadow of death which man fears is only a shadow. For once a man stares that shadow of death in the face, he will be able to see past it and discover the other side.

PERVERSION

WHY PORN TURNS EVERYTHING KINKY

A viewer will often try to avoid the emotional hangover by perpetuating the high. He will sit in a dark room surfing the internet for hours, focusing all his attention on the screen. This kind of chronic viewing will not keep him satisfied. The efficacy of the pornographic drug only declines with use. It never remains constant. After a while, those naked bodies will start to look boring. Plain "vanilla" sex will not carry the same appeal anymore. Repeated exposure to this material desensitizes the mind. As a guy develops a tolerance for what he is watching, he will need more intense images to feel the same high. His sexual desires will then begin to turn kinky.

> "WHO BEING PAST FEELING, HAVE GIVEN THEMSELVES OVER TO LEWDNESS, TO WORK ALL UNCLEANNESS WITH GREEDINESS."
> EPHES 4:19, NKJV

The porn industry knows this kind of desensitization occurs. It tries to accommodate the viewer's changing tastes by pushing the limits. Hard core pornography dabbles in every type of sexual deviancy. The depths these films plunge into can be shocking to the conscience. Producers will deliberately create this shock value to keep the high going, but this never works for long. Desensitization only sets in again and the urge for even darker content emerges. With every line crossed, the viewer's tastes spiral downward. One perverse thing leads to another. This frantic search for satisfaction perpetuates a vicious cycle of perversion.

"GOD GAVE THEM OVER TO A DEBASED MIND."
ROM 1:28, NKJV

Researchers have found the chronic viewing of porn does degrade the brain. MRI scans have shown that the brain's gray matter shrinks over time when exposed to large amounts of porn. (Hilton, 2013)[11] A man's higher cognitive functions deteriorates with exposure. His perception distorts. The brain's circuitry is neuroplastic and will change with different types of stimuli. It can be reprogrammed to like all sorts of twisted things. Normal feelings of sexual attraction can be distorted into something unnatural.

> "AS SODOM AND GOMORRAH, AND THE CITIES
> AROUND THEM IN A SIMILAR MANNER TO THESE,
> HAVING GIVEN THEMSELVES OVER TO SEXUAL
> IMMORALITY AND GONE AFTER STRANGE FLESH..."
> JUDE 1:7, NKJV

Bizarre and grotesque fetishes can be seen growing prominent in the culture. Unhealthy behaviors like drinking urine, eating feces, and consuming blood are beginning to gain acceptance. Young, hypersexualized individuals are emulating these deviant behaviors. Some have lost their attraction for women altogether preferring animals, cartoon characters, or even inanimate objects. People imitate what they glorify. Little by little, their cultural tastes are being transformed by porn's messaging. Criminal studies have reported many convicted pedophiles "had no previous interest" in their deviant behavior until viewing child pornography.(Heather Wood, 2013)[12] These criminals felt compelled to act out their heinous deeds. The pheromone effect of the perverted novelty was the only thing that kept their high going. Does anyone really want to plague themselves with any of these kinds of vile passions?

> "FOR THIS REASON, GOD GAVE THEM UP TO VILE PASSIONS."
> ROM 1:26, NKJV

Behind this urge to get dirty lies a desire for something deeper. The graphic example of oral sex can prove this point. Fellatio is a common perversion found in many pornographic scenes. It is very popular scene to watch among guys. The physical mechanics alone should stir a natural aversion in everyone. Afterall, a woman doesn't enjoy gagging herself on a male's private part nor does a man enjoy grating his most sensitive member across a female's sharp teeth. But these harsh realities do not always register with a porn viewer fixated by the screen. He can look past these displeasures because he does not experience them firsthand. In fact, he is looking past most of what is seen on the screen.

A guy does not watch a fellatio scene to stare at other men's penises. He does not even watch it to see a naked woman either. In a fellatio scene, the camera shot focuses on the woman's face. It is not the unbecoming facial expressions that make the scene so appealing to men. The woman's emotional reactions to the man's penis is what makes the scene powerful. She adores the very thing that makes him male. This zeal in stooping to where few others would venture is perceived as a physical manifestation of love. It is this sensation that causes the ecstatic feelings in a guy and makes the scene so appealing. The porn viewer is seeing love in the dirty deed. This ecstatic experience causes a shift in his perception. Now whenever the desire to re-experience love comes on, a guy will think of the dirty deed as the means of obtaining it.

"BUT IT HAS HAPPENED TO THEM ACCORDING TO
THE TRUE PROVERB: A DOG RETURNS TO HIS OWN
VOMIT, AND A SOW, HAVING WASHED, TO HER
WALLOWING IN THE MIRE."
II PETER 2:22, NKJV

This confusion between dirty deeds and loving acts causes people to acquire some very vile passions. The initial aftereffects of watching such a perverted thing may leave a viewer with a sick feeling inside, but those reactions do subside. People do begin liking the perverted elements in time. Don't underestimate Porn's ability to glamorize the vile and get their audiences to start liking it. Those things that would make a dog vomit at first can begin to look yummy.

Porn producers know how to condition a viewer's tastes. Cognitive conditioning is a well-known psychological technique discovered by Ivan Pavlov. With cognitive conditioning, Pavlov learned a dog could be trained to salivate over almost anything. When a guy thinks with his penis, he does not reason any better than a dog. Hormonal stimulus impairs his rational thought. This is why a man must be careful with what he consumes with his eyes. If a guy masturbates to any of these perverted images, the associations will be reinforced in his head. It will program the learned behavior into muscle memory and make the perversion second nature.

DEFILEMENT

HOW PORN RUINS A MAN'S SEX LIFE

"WHAT COMES OUT OF A MAN, THAT DEFILES A MAN. FOR FROM WITHIN, OUT OF THE HEART OF MEN, PROCEED EVIL THOUGHTS...ALL THESE EVIL THINGS COME FROM WITHIN AND DEFILE A MAN."
MARK 7:20-23 NKJV

Nobody ever tries to ruin their own sex life on purpose, but a perverted person does not know any better. He cannot think clearly and so cannot course correct. Those perverted thoughts become the man's stumbling block. At this point, a man's own perverted feelings spill over into the real world and start creating real-life consequences for him. This is why perversion always leads to defilement. For whatever is internalized and nurtured in the heart will eventually materialize into a person's life. Again, wherever the heart points, there the whole person must go. A ruined mind leads to the ruin of everything else.

> "WOE TO HIM WHO...LOOKS ON HIS NAKEDNESS!
> YOU ARE FILLED WITH SHAME INSTEAD OF GLORY.
> YOU ALSO...BE EXPOSED..."
> HAB 2:15-16, NKJV

It is easy for the public to recognize this when it occurs. For when a guy does not control his own eyeballs, his own hormones burn out of control. Those raging hormones impair his ability to relate with the opposite sex. A guy obsessed with sex does not see himself approaching women; he does not see his own embarrassing behavior. How his eyes bug out, how he shakes with excitement, and how drool starts dripping from his mouth. A guy with sex on his brain just can't play it cool. Overexcitement makes it impossible for him to be smooth, natural, or even sexy. He struggles to compose himself and form coherent words. The guy stumbles all over and makes a complete fool of himself.

> "NOW I WILL UNCOVER HER LEWDNESS IN THE SIGHT OF HER LOVERS..."
> HOSEA 2:10, NKJV

A woman can tell when a guy is only after one thing; she can smell the desperation a mile away. Sexual neediness is not an attractive trait. It broadcasts an "I-am-not-worthy" tone to all the women in the room. The creepy vibes spook them and cause them to run away. The guy will repel every beautiful woman and will not understand why. He is stuck in his own head and unable to connect. Daydreaming about his own sexual fantasies has put him under a spiritual trance.

"SHE WILL CHASE HER LOVERS, BUT NOT OVERTAKE THEM."
HOSEA 2:7, NKJV

Of course, a guy with an inward obsession won't be able to take the hint. He will chase the girl around attempting to keep her from getting away. He will exasperate himself going overboard on the affection. He will become clingy and will not afford his cherished woman any breathing space. This persistent pestering will make him a nuisance. A guy who acts like this will find he won't be able to win the affection of any beautiful woman to save his life. Every romantic gesture made will be seen with a string attached. Females will work together to avoid such unsavory individuals. They will send out text messages alerting all their female friends when such a guy enters the room. God never gives someone more than they can handle. If a woman's looks are too hot for someone to handle, she will be placed out of his league.

> "FOR A HARLOT IS A DEEP PIT, AND A SEDUCTRESS IS A NARROW WELL. SHE ALSO LIES IN WAIT AS FOR A VICTIM AND INCREASES THE UNFAITHFUL AMONG MEN."
> PROV 23:27-28, NKJV

Of course, not all women run away from the guy who lacks restraint. Some women don't mind letting their body do all the talking. By wearing some provocative dress, these women are deliberately trying to lure a man into their trap. The Bible describes these kinds of women as snares and the world is filled with them. A guy won't suspect her unspoken promise of sex will devolve into a sexless hell. For a woman's real personality always comes out and nobody can stand being around an ugly character for too long. This repulsion for one's true character will always kill the mood.

> " IMMEDIATELY HE WENT AFTER HER, AS AN OX
> GOES TO THE SLAUGHTER."
> PROV 7:22, NKJV

A guy who can't control his eyes will never be able to find the right woman. Finding her would require navigating through a myriad of pretty faces. He would fall for the first pretty face he sees; he would fall for the boobie trap. A guy who lacks self-control has no ability to filter. His inclination to focus on a woman's body blinds him to the heart. If the heart does not matter to a guy, he will find himself trapped by someone heartless.

> "... COME TOGETHER AGAIN SO THAT SATAN DOES
> NOT TEMPT YOU BECAUSE OF YOUR LACK OF SELF-
> CONTROL."
> I COR 7:5, NKJV

A pornographic mind not only makes it hard to relate with and filter out women, it also makes it hard to sexually perform. Erections and ejaculating are not voluntary reflexes like moving an arm at will. A man's entire sexual performance flows from his desire. His erection grows from being sexually aroused. His penis ejaculates as these desires peak and his erection diminishes as these passions subside. A man's penis and heart are linked. His feelings act like a control switchboard to the whole process. If a guy does not have his desires under control, he will not have control of his penis either.

"BUT THE FRUIT OF THE SPIRIT IS...SELF CONTROL."
GAL 5:22-23, NKJV

Male overexcitement causes premature ejaculation. A guy carrying around a bunch of pornographic images in his head remains in a heightened state of sexual tension. Impure thoughts make him like a boiling tea kettle ready to blow. The slightest added stimulus will set him

119

off. This heightened sexual tension makes it hard to control one's urges. A guy suffering from premature ejaculation will lack stamina in the bedroom. He will struggle to last longer than a couple of thrusts. In many cases, sex will be over before it even starts. Premature ejaculation deprives a guy from the ability to enjoy a partner and please her in bed.

> "...HE WHO COMMITS SEXUAL IMMORALITY SINS AGAINST HIS OWN BODY."
> I COR 6:18, NKJV

Sexual Desensitization is what causes erectile dysfunction (ED). As the heart desensitizes to all the overstimulation, the normal stimulus of a naked woman will no longer be able to give a man an erection anymore. He won't be able to get hard from seeing his naked wife. His body will be conditioned to all the extreme stimulation found in hard-core pornography. He will now need those bizarre fetishes just to get his kicks off. Being excited by anything else will become a struggle. Scientific studies and surveys support this positive correlation between chronic porn use and male sexual dysfunction. (Bothe, 2021) Online testimonials also confirm this finding. (Anti Pornography.org, n.d.) [14]

> "...BLESSED IS HE WHO WATCHES, AND KEEPS HIS GARMENTS, LEST HE WALK NAKED AND THEY SEE HIS SHAME."
> REV 16:15, NKJV

For a guy, the inability to last long or even get an erection creates lots of performance anxiety. A guy doesn't want to see the disappointment on a partner's face. His fear of failing will only exacerbate the problems. To avoid any humiliation, he will often choose to sideline himself and not venture into any sexual encounter with a woman at all. This is how performance anxiety leads to sexual inhibition.

Those impure pornographic thoughts are what keep a guy out of step with his partner. The longer someone watches porn, the more these physical and emotional defilements progress.

> "MARRIAGE IS HONORABLE AMONG ALL, AND THE BED UNDEFILED; BUT FORNICATORS AND ADULTERERS GOD WILL JUDGE."
> HEB 13:4, NKJV

A man should never bring any kind of pornography into the bedroom. Three is a crowd in the marriage bed. The visual images will only steal away a guy's attention and a woman will sense when her partner's heart is somewhere else. This awareness will only kill the emotional experience for her. A woman cannot compete with a fantasy. The exaggerated images will only play on a woman's insecurities and instill a sense of inadequacy. A man never wins making a woman lose. Heightening a woman's inhibitions will only make opening up and connecting harder than ever.

> "LET HIM KISS ME WITH THE KISSES OF HIS MOUTH-
> FOR YOUR LOVE IS BETTER THAN WINE."
> SONG 1:2, NKJV

A woman has sex to get love. She gets off on being loved. Her vagina gets wet and opens from experiencing real love. Just like a man, a woman's heart and sexual parts are linked. If a man wants to gain access to a woman's body, he must put her in the mood. He does this by bringing his own full heart into the experience. It is the man's love for the woman's beauty that creates all those fireworks. To perform well a man must possess purity of heart. A calm and collect spirit is the key to remaining in the moment and lasting through the entire experience.

> "INDEED, I WILL CAST HER INTO A SICKBED,
> AND THOSE WHO COMMIT ADULTERY WITH HER
> INTO GREAT TRIBULATION..."
> REV 2:22, NKJV

Again, Sex can be a wonderful thing if done right, but it can also be a terrible thing if done wrong. Never try to force a woman into doing something she is not comfortable with. Don't subject her to any kind of degrading treatment that dehumanizes her or violates social norms. It will only create a negative reaction in the woman. It will never inspire the female love that men want. Without love, the sexual act is stripped of magic. If a woman is not given sufficient emotional stimulation, she will lack the lubrication needed for intercourse. This will make the physical act more painful than pleasurable. It will turn the bed of roses into a bed of suffering.

"...HER RULERS DEARLY LOVE DISHONOR."
Hosea 4:18, NKJV

A man should not try to groom his partner into playing the part of some pornographic perversion. He should never try to incorporate any perverted thing into his lovemaking. A man is bound to have his expectations dashed if he tries. Reality will pop his bubble. Perversions are not an attractive thing. They can only ruin lovemaking; they will not spice up a couple's love life. Countless females complain on-line about being pressured to act out their boyfriend's weird fetish. The twisted kinks shocked, horrified, and repulsed them. Perversion will forever change how a woman feels about her partner. Something is wrong with the perverted person and now that special someone knows about it. The same perversion that defiles a man's heart and body will also defile his reputation. To peddle kinks is to embrace dishonor.

> "...THE MEN LEAVING THE NATURAL USE OF THE WOMAN, BURNED IN THEIR LUST...COMMITTING WHAT IS SHAMEFUL AND RECEIVING IN THEMSELVES THE PENALTY OF THEIR ERROR..."
> ROM 1:27, NKJV

A man should never allow any of these bizarre fetishes to get locked into his head. Porn's perversion and defilement will emasculate a man and turn him into a reprobate. A guy becomes what he watches. If he watches child porn, he will become a pedophile. If he watches BDSM, he will become a sadist. Remember anyone who sins sexually sins against his own body. Nobody gets around this. To indulge in perversion is to defile oneself. Anyone foolish enough to act out that perversion will only receive within themselves the penalty of their error.

"THEY SHALL NOT TAKE A WIFE WHO
IS A HARLOT OR A DEFILED WOMAN…"
LEV 21:7, NKJV

Don't think turning to some anonymous street prostitute from skid row will somehow change things to a more desirable outcome. A street girl doesn't enjoy being defiled any more than the average woman. In fact, prostitutes come to hate their clients because of these experiences. They would be even less inclined to save a man's reputation. A woman who has been around the block and who is willing to do any kinky thing for a price will come with a sordid sexual history. She would be sharing more than just 'the love' with her clients. Don't go into any of these types of women. Anyone trying to scour the bottom of the barrel to find pleasure is in for a rude awakening. Bad ideas have consequences. Just going thru the physical motions will not create the stars a guy hopes for.

ABOMINATION

PORN FOSTERS HATE RATHER THAN LOVE

"THE HATRED WITH WHICH HE HATED HER
WAS GREATER THAN THE LOVE WITH WHICH HE
HAD LOVED HER."
II SAM 13:15, NKJV

After the sirens on the screen tease and torture a viewer until he can't bear it anymore. After they warp his mind and twist his desires so much, he begins acting out in a way that defiles his body leaving him a lonely, emasculated, impotent, and infected mess. What will the man's emotional reaction to all this be? He will come to resent all the aggravation and heartache. He will want to take his anger out on someone. He will not blame himself for being taken by the images in pornography. He won't even blame the devil for tempting him to look. He will blame the women for what has been done to him. He will come to hate all women for his troubles. Pornography breeds misogyny in the culture. It incites hatred rather than love. For this reason, Pornography can be characterized as an abomination.

"WHERE DO WARS AND FIGHT COME FROM AMONG YOU? DO THEY NOT COME FROM YOUR DESIRES FOR PLEASURE THAT WAR IN YOUR MEMBERS? YOU LUST AND DO NOT HAVE..."
JAMES 4:1-2, NKJV

Porn producers know watching their films aggravates the male psyche. To placate that irritation a bit, producers will incorporate verbal and physical abuse toward women into their scenes. One out of every eight porn site titles have been found to promote acts of sexual violence. (Vera-Gray, 2021) Researchers have suggested that as many as 9 in 10 porn scenes contain some form of physical violence or aggression. (Fritz, 2020) The spectrum of abuse can vary from spanking a girl for being "naughty" to extreme forms where the woman is subjected to various types of torture. Porn will try to make the ill treatment seem more palatable to the conscience by dehumanizing the girls. (Zhou, 2021) It will also encourage the aggression in males by depicting the violence as something desirable to women. Researchers have found in 95% of these scenes, the recipient of that violence responded with pleasure (Bridges, 2010)

"...THEIR SOUL DELIGHTS IN THEIR ABOMINATIONS..."
ISA 66:3, NKJV

Initial exposure to these sadistic elements does bother the male psyche. Men were designed to love women and not hate them. Nobody would want to see their wife, mother, sister, or daughter treated in such fashion. Deep down, a guy understands every female is someone's family member. Nevertheless, the pain of chronic teasing does chip away at a man's sensitivities. This is why even the non-violent scenes can be said to incite aggression in males. A guy driven crazy by what he sees will become sexually frustrated and will grow accustomed to liking those hateful elements.

"DO NOT ENVY THE VIOLENT OR CHOOSE ANY OF
THEIR WAYS."
PROV 3:31, NIV

Painting sexual aggression as some sort of manly thing imprints a terrible idea into the mind of a young man. To a guy, the ability to fight and to love are both seen as rites of passage into manhood. It can feel manly to win the affection of a woman. It can also feel manly to exert one's dominance over another opponent. Both feats

131

will create an emotional high in a guy. The porn narrative intermingles these sensations together. Blurring the line between male assertiveness and sexual aggression. This type of messaging will condition a guy to get off on sexual aggression and transform him into something bad. It will conflate becoming a man with becoming a monster.

> "My Son, if sinners entice you, Do not consent."
> Prov 1:10, NKJV

At first, a boy with sensitivities toward the feelings of others may hold reservations about being so aggressive toward women. Deep down, he loves women and doesn't want to hurt them. He resists the toxic message and shuts down for a while. From an emotional standpoint, this is all a man can do. In the culture, anger is considered the only emotion a guy can express without being ridiculed by outsiders. Porn's messaging will characterize a young man's hesitancy as some sort of lack of confidence on his part. His sensitivity will be equated with somehow being less of a man.

> "FOR THEY LOVED THE PRAISE OF MEN MORE THAN THE PRAISE OF GOD."
> JOHN 12:43, NKJV

Male viewers internalize this message whether they like it or not. Whenever a guy gets nowhere with a woman and she responds with the words "you are too nice," porn's message will once again ring into his ears- a guy is not man enough until he is mean. Getting praised for being the "nice guy" will not soothe the rejected man's ego. A growing sexual frustration inside will begin to eat at him and break down his initial resistance to the perverted message changing the desire to score into a desire to strike.

"AS IN WATER FACE REFLECTS FACE,
SO A MAN'S HEART REVEALS THE MAN."
PROV 27:19, NKJV

The fetish for sadomasochism (BDSM) exhibits this alarming trend taking shape within the culture. The BDSM community may not equate their own desires with any kind of malicious intent. In their mind, nobody wants to really hurt someone else. At least, these people tell themselves this. They don't see their fetish as leading anywhere. They are not reflecting on their true feelings. If a person had no real desire to hurt anyone, then why even pretend about it? Just the desire to roleplay like this should tell a person something. The sadomasochist is not looking at where his own compass needle is pointing. He does not understand where his life is headed. He is undergoing a metamorphosis and does not know it.

"THEN WHEN DESIRE HAS CONCEIVED, IT GIVES
BIRTH TO SIN; AND SIN WHEN IT IS FULL GROWN,
BRINGS FORTH DEATH."
JAMES 1:15, NKJV

Perversion is a gradual process. It often escapes the individual's notice until someone else points it out. Under the cloak of cover, it can grow unabated. These violent perversions can progress beyond roleplaying. Darker versions of these BDSM themes do exist on the dark web- an illegal form of pornography referred to as the snuff film; it is called this because the sexual scene culminates in the death of a person. Their life being snuffed out in some gruesome way for the sheer pleasure of an audience. If allowed to go on long enough, porn's cycle of perversion can culminate in a twisted desire to murder.

"DO NOT PROSTITUTE YOUR DAUGHTER, TO CAUSE
HER TO BE A HARLOT, LEST THE LAND FALL INTO
HARLOTRY, AND THE LAND BECOME FULL OF
WICKEDNESS."
LEV 19:29, NKJV

Nobody can say these types of films don't exist or that there are not people out there who enjoy these things. In 2000, the Guardian paper reported how MI5, Britian's counter-intelligence service, busted a child porn ring out of Russia peddling films showing young kids being mutilated in a sadistic fashion as entertainment. (Burke, 2000)[22] In the raid, three thousand films were intercepted. Many of these videos depicted children being killed on camera. The incident set off a manhunt for buyers who were paying anywhere between £50 and £100 for the material across several countries. There are people in the world who have learned to get their kicks off of death. Scores of sexual perpetrators have even been caught making their own personal snuff footage. (Brubaker, 2015) [23]

"...DO NOT LEARN TO IMITATE THE DETESTABLE
WAYS OF THE NATIONS THERE."
DT 18:9, NIV

Consuming these kinds of films does instill a compulsion to act them out. Eventually, a viewer will grow discontent from just pretending. When the feelings of dissatisfaction take over and get the best of someone, the monster inside can no longer be kept under control. It is then that the egg hatches. The person often blows up out of nowhere. It is as if a switch flips and that other part of oneself just comes out. When this happens, a victim's pleas for help will fall on deaf ears. Survivors have labeled their perpetrators as "sociopaths" because they were incapable of feeling. An individual caught up in his own head can't sympathize with the plight of someone else. He will be described as an individual who had fallen under a trance.

> "…SIR, DID YOU NOT SOW GOOD SEED IN YOUR
> FIELD?
> HOW THEN DOES IT HAVE TARES?
> HE SAID TO THEM, 'AN ENEMY HAS DONE THIS'…"
> MT 13:27-28, NKJV

Criminal psychologists will study this kind of behavior. To see what drives a person to indulge in such horrific acts. Profilers have found all these cases follow a few noticeable patterns. Every perpetrator is trying to live out a fantasy. They want to be able to use their victims in whatever way seems fit to them, but personal volition gets in the way of this. Therefore, the perpetrator will coerce, kidnap, torture, and even murder their victim to gain that complete access.

"YOU ARE OF YOUR FATHER THE DEVIL,
AND THE DESIRES OF YOUR FATHER YOU WANT TO
DO."
JOHN 8:44, NKJV

For the perpetrator, death is no longer just a means to an end, but a process to be enjoyed. These depraved individuals come to enjoy watching those explicit acts of violence, torture, and death. Many will record their own heinous crimes on film. If they can't film it, they will try to collect some sort of keepsake or memento to remember the incident by. They want to relive the experience over and over in their head.

"THEY DO NOT DIRECT THEIR DEEDS TOWARD
TURNING TO THEIR GOD,
FOR THE SPIRIT OF HARLOTRY IS IN THEIR
MIDST..."
HOSEA 5:4, NKJV

After it is all over, Police and eyewitnesses have reported feeling creepy vibes around these heinous crime scenes. Criminal investigators have learned to use these sensations as leads for detecting when something is not right. Police will interrogate these individuals to see what possessed them to do such heinous things. Their response will often be "I don't know what came over me." The perpetrator was not himself, but this does not absolve him of any responsibility. For he became a willing vessel of evil.

"...THE SERPENT DECEIVED ME, AND I ATE."
GEN 3:13, NKJV

Many rapists and serial killers will attribute their own behavior to the perverting influences of pornography. Watching over long periods of time changed these people for the worse and groomed them to do many of the terrible things they did. Nobody starts out as a reprobate. They were made that way from the inside out. Of course, not everyone who has watches porn slides this far down the perversion scale and plunges into this level of depravity. But if that seed implanted within the mind gets watered and nurtured, it most certainly will germinate and sprout forth. The desire to kill is the end of the road for every man who fails to stop looking.

LOVE

HOW IT CREATES ALL THE MAGIC

"YOU WORSHIP WHAT YOU DO NOT KNOW…"
JOHN 4:22, NKJV

If a guy has any hope of stemming this tide of negative consequences, he is going to have to grapple with the emotional draw pulling him in. Most guys don't really understand Love. Their confusion about Love keeps them looking in the wrong place. To the average guy, Love is an abstraction; an idea he cannot wrap his mind around. Tracing out the abstraction could train his eye to see and remove the scales. It would guide him into a better place.

"BUT KING SOLOMON LOVED MANY FOREIGN
WOMEN…"
I KINGS 11:1, NKJV

What is it about the porn star that makes a
guy see stars? In terms of outward looks, she is
not more beautiful than the average woman. As
mentioned before, she does likes sex more than
the average woman. A porn star never just lays
there like a martyr; she does not have sex out of
compulsion or some sense of duty. Her eagerness
and active participation demonstrate that she
loves the activity just as much as her male
counterpart. From the outward looks of it, she is
a nymphomaniac.

"FOR THE LIPS OF AN IMMORAL WOMAN DRIP
HONEY AND HER MOUTH IS SMOOTHER THAN OIL."
PROV 5:3, NKJV

Why does a guy come away with this
impression? Her words may be graphic, but these
phrases in themselves are not what does it.

143

Afterall, words can feel contrived at times (especially if overdone). In many cases, the porn stars words are not even legible. This does not matter to a man. How a woman talks matters more than what she says. The porn star's guttural cooing and moaning make the strongest impression. Afterall, intense feelings can't always be put into words. The guy is reading between the lines to sense those emotions within her voice. The heart behind her words are what really matter. The tone within her voice conveys her passionate feelings and spirit.

"DO NOT LUST AFTER HER BEAUTY IN YOUR HEART, NOR LET HER ALLURE YOU WITH HER EYELIDS."
PROV 6:25, NKJV

When the porn star looks into the camera, the look on her face speak volumes. The guy is seeing more than what is visible. He is looking into her eyes and peering into her soul. He is trying to discover those spiritual qualities within her- the ghost within the machine. Sexual intimacy is more about seeing the spirit within than anything else. A guy cares about what a woman is thinking and feeling. He is trying to gauge what she is feeling from her expressions. The viewer is attempting to ascertain if the woman is exhibiting real spirit in the bedroom. He is trying to sense the woman's spirit within.

"WHOEVER COMMITS ADULTERY WITH A WOMAN LACKS UNDERSTANDING..."
PROV 6:32, NKJV

Of course, a porn star gives the male viewer plenty of material to work with. Everything from how she holds herself to how she spreads her legs exhibits a zealous passion. The porn star seems to put her whole heart into what she is doing. Her every mannerism conveys her motives. Her gestures seethe with passionate sentiment. This sexual passion animates her body. A woman who bears her body and soul like this is truly a sight to see. She is a type of love manifested in the flesh.

"HOW FAIR IS YOUR LOVE...HOW MUCH BETTER THAN WINE IS YOUR LOVE..."
SONG 4:10, NKJV

It is this visual manifestation of love that catches the man's eye. The porn star's sexual feelings stir an exhilarating vibe within him. His heart begins to thump. This sensation will stop a guy in his tracks. Most guys have never seen such a vivid expression of love before. The experience leaves him smitten. Deep down a guy wants a woman who loves like that. She is a kindred spirit. A woman who desires to have sex with him just as much as he desires to have sex with her. This characteristic gives her an almost magical quality. The porn star embodies the kind of love a man dreams about.

"...YOU HAVE RAVISHED MY HEART
WITH ONE LOOK OF YOUR EYES..."
PROV 7:18, NKJV

This is why a man's heart is drawn to seeing those pornographic images. He is trying to get a glimpse of that love once again. The man dreams of being loved by that woman on the screen. His heart yearns to feel that love once again. His eyes will wander all over the internet just to find that right image; the one that will put his mind into a tailspin and set his passions ablaze. The man is really chasing an emotional experience. He is choosing to leave the real world behind and suspend his disbelief just to feel these sensations. Before long, his spirit is soaring. In truth, the viewer is really seeking a certain spiritual state.

> "AND YOU SHALL GROPE AT NOONDAY, AS A BLIND
> MAN GROPES IN DARKNESS..."
> DT 28:29, NKJV

Because a guy does not really understand what he is grasping for, he will use his feelings as a gauge or a divining rod to find it. Anything that causes butterflies within his gut will cause him to stop and take notice. This may not be the best method, but a guy lacking knowledge has no other indicator to go on. He fumbles around and chases every sensation that bedazzles. To a guy, the feelings become proof. Of course, holding on to those emotional goosebumps becomes hard if a person doesn't really understand what causes those pleasurable sensations.

> "...GOD IS LOVE."
> I JOHN 4:8, NKJV

Love is more than just a physical feeling. Those feelings just don't happen anymore than trees swaying back and forth in the wind or leaves floating in mid-air by themselves. An Invisible agent is responsible for creating those effects. God is Love; He is the one who creates all the magic. To feel real Love simply means to perceive His Spirit.

"BECAUSE YOUR LOVE IS BETTER THAN LIFE..."
Ps 63:3, NIV

Most guys would never think of God as their own source of sexual fulfillment. In their eyes, a man's desire to orgasm is seen more as a physical urge than anything else. Some self-reflection can easily disprove this belief. None of the physical manifestations associated with the orgasm are what men find appealing about it. It is not the funny faces and grimacing in angst that makes the physical orgasm attractive. Nor is it the labored breathing, the moaning, the grunting, the gasping, or the screaming in an erratic fashion. Most people don't like losing control in front of others

149

where their body tenses up, arches, and convulses. For most, losing control and wetting oneself in public can be rather embarrassing. This is why people prefer to have their orgasms in private. Outsiders who don't know what is occurring might wonder what was happening to someone with their eyes rolling back into their head. Orgasmic people who spasm and twitch in an involuntary manner look like they are possessed; they look like that because they are.

"...THEY HAVE FORSAKEN ME,
THE FOUNTAIN OF LIVING WATERS..."
JER 2:13, NKJV

Those feelings of love inside are what people are getting off on- the real manifestation of God's presence. When a man and woman come together in love, God's Spirit can be found within the midst of them. The emotional pleasures the man and woman feel in this state are the byproduct of having God's Spirit stirring within. God is the fountain of living water. As those waves of pleasure inside build to a peak, streams of living water literally flow from their loins. All sex addicts have felt these effects before, they just never knew what caused all those feelings inside. To be orgasmic is to be in a Spiritual State.

SPIRITUAL FULFILLMENT

WHEN THE CRAVINGS END

"...YOU ARE A SWIFT DROMEDARY...THAT SNIFFS AT
THE WIND IN HER DESIRE."
JER 2:23-24, NKJV

On screen, the porn star exhibits real spirit in the bedroom. She puts her heart into what she is doing. She throws her back into it like she means it. To witness her in action stirs the most glorious feelings inside. The viewer thinks he has found love. He believes the woman on the screen is causing all those pleasurable butterflies in his gut. Men crave to experience those feelings over and over. It is this desire for those feelings that makes pornography so hard to give up.

"...ALL WAS VANITY AND GRASPING FOR THE
WIND..."
Ecc 2:11, NKJV

The porn viewer yearns to find a real woman like this. He scans the horizon looking for his dream girl; he searches the world over and never finds her. Why is this the case? That woman is a figment of his imagination. Pornographic images are nothing more than a false image- a mirage. The façade always fades upon closer inspection. If a guy were to date one of these "dream girls", the real person inside would only come to dispel the first impression. As this real character comes into focus, the man would start to realize such a woman was not what he had dreamed of. He would then begin to wonder what he ever saw in the object of his affection.

"...BUT MY PEOPLE HAVE CHANGED THEIR GLORY
FOR WHAT DOES NOT PROFIT..."
JER 2:11, NKJV

The man does not realize he is projecting his own fantasies on to strangers. He is mistaking his own spiritual projection for the reality. When a man discovers that the real woman in front of him is not his desire, his eyes will start to wander back to porn once again. The man is in love with a dream. He has fallen in love with an image and will find it hard to settle for anything less. Therefore, he can never settle down. He will continue to search for the woman of his dreams. He can't rest until she materializes.

"THEREFORE, PUT TO DEATH YOUR MEMBERS
WHICH ARE ON THE EARTH: FORNICATION,
UNCLEANNESS, PASSION, EVIL DESIRE, AND
COVETOUSNESS,
WHICH IS IDOLATRY."
COL 3:5, NKJV

Please know chasing these kinds of phantoms are a hopeless futility. The path never leads anywhere good. A false image could never bring a man any kind of lasting satisfaction. A wise man knows better than to chase mirages. Even if the heat of the desert makes him thirsty, he knows better than to waste precious energy chasing after foolishness. The thrill of the chase is the only fleeting pleasure to be gained from such a pursuit. A wise man recognizes the mirage for what it is. His right perception safeguards him from doing anything foolish. Instead of chasing facades, He focuses his efforts on what really satisfies- how to make the wet dream a reality. A wise man knows the fantasy alone could never satisfy. Truly living the dream will require a man to leave the dream world.

> "...BUT THOSE WHO CHASE FANTASIES HAVE NO
> SENSE."
> PROV 12:11, NIV

The porn viewer can't seem to help himself though. He still can't help but think there is someone out there who might fulfill his wildest dreams. He pours over a myriad of images looking for that someone that will titillate his senses. He is looking for a woman who will possess the right kind of chemistry; someone who can provide that spark and ignite those passionate feelings inside. He prefer strangers over anyone familiar. The anonymity leaves room for the imagination to run wild. In truth, the man is not looking for any one person; he is seeking out a feeling- something that will fill up his senses. The man's pursuit of pleasure is really the hunt for a spiritual high. He does not realize it yet, but he is seeking spiritual fulfillment.

"[THEY] CHANGED THE GLORY OF THE INCORRUPTIBLE GOD INTO AN IMAGE MADE LIKE CORRUPTIBLE MAN..."
ROM 1:23, NKJV

Of course, the porn viewer does not make any distinction between what is seen on the screen and what is felt in his heart. He simply attributes those emotions he feels to the woman on the screen. This is why he wants to see her again. He is hoping that by seeing her again, it will bring him more pleasure. What a man really wants is to feel more of those pleasurable sensations inside. But those magical feelings are not a physical phenomenon; they are a spiritual manifestation. Spirits create those internal fireworks. The very qualities a man is looking for in a potential mate are those same attributes found in God's Spirit.

The search for a partner and the quest for God are the same pursuit.

"SURELY, AS A WIFE TREACHEROUSLY DEPARTS FROM HER HUSBAND, SO HAVE YOU DEALT TREACHEROUSLY WITH ME..."
JER 3:20, NKJV

Of course, a man will never find God looking at pornography. Idols kick God off the pedestal of one's heart. Whenever a man goes off to enjoy porn, he is running out on God. God always sees what a man does in the dark. He equates the man's idolatry with a sexually immoral act. His reaction closely resembles those same feelings a jealous husband might have toward an unfaithful wife. He will abandon the man with idols in his heart. This is why the porn viewer always feels hollow afterward. God's absence leaves a noticeable vacuum.

"...THEN I ALIENATED MYSELF FROM HER..."
EZEK 23:18, NKJV

In a very real sense, pornography does suck the life right out of a person. God's absence wrecks a man's emotional state. All the good feelings drain away; only an empty feeling inside remains. The vacuous state destroys a man's soul- the seat of his emotions. This is why a terrible low follows the immense high. Most men think little about their own soul before watching. They won't really appreciate what is lost until it is gone.

"THEY SHALL GO TO SEEK THE LORD, BUT THEY WILL NOT FIND HIM; HE HAS WITHDRAWN HIMSELF FROM THEM."
HOSEA 5:6, NKJV

A guy who finds himself in this predicament will know something has been lost. For none of the typical amusements generate the same desired effects anymore. Favorite past times stop being fun. Foods begin to lose their flavor. Nothing seems to satisfy anymore. Everything starts to feel dead and empty inside. This inability to derive joy out of anything creates a great deal of frustration. A guy will want to escape these stresses. The inability to cope will make him desperate. He will return to the only source of pleasure he knows left-the pornography itself. For nothing else seems to make him feel good and he cannot put his finger on why.

"WHEN YOU CRY OUT, LET YOUR COLLECTION OF IDOLS DELIVER YOU..."
ISA 57:13, NKJV

The spiritual void is what makes an individual prone to addiction. God leaves the unfaithful person to his idols. As a result, the man must now turn to them for satisfaction. Because the porn viewer finds enjoyment in nothing else, he will come to depend upon his viewing high just to get by. The idea of going without will now make him feel anxious. For he does not know how to live without his emotional crutch. The need to feel good causes him to obsess over it. A porn addiction feels like an immovable obstacle for a reason. The addictive urges never went away because the need for love never goes away. The withdrawal pains were the body's way of trying to communicate a real need. Until the spiritual void gets filled again, those cravings won't ever subside.

> "THEIR SORROWS SHALL BE MULTIPLIED WHO HASTEN AFTER ANOTHER GOD..."
> Ps 16:4, NKJV

A guy will try to keep the magical feelings going by continuing to watch. In the process, he will only dig himself deeper into a spiritual rut. Porn deprives a man of every other passion he might have had in life. His vitality, vigor, and sense of purpose will all be lost. How does a person get excited over something that does not bring him pleasure anymore? Life without love is an empty existence. The addict has lost his passion for living. This loss of all enjoyment turns his heart into an empty coffin. The man's eyes will start to exhibit a lifelessness to everyone around him. He has become 'a man without a chest' as C.S. Lewis would say. Pornography has turned him into a shell of a person.

> "...HE WHO LOVES HIS WIFE LOVES HIMSELF."
> EPHES 5:28, NKJV

A man can't give a woman what he does not have. He can't enliven anyone if he himself feels dead inside. Pornography deprives a man of the ability to win with women. Women are not attracted to desperate individuals; they have no interest in filling a man's spiritual void. When a guy begins to realize he is unable to escape these terrible circumstances, a spiritual gloom will start to creep in. The man will confine himself to his room and immerses himself into the computer screen. A guy who looks at porn doesn't know how to win with women. Lack of understanding hinders his progress. He scrolls through a myriad of websites because he doesn't know how to get what he wants from the woman in his life. He must settle for watching other people live out their dreams from the sidelines. The view only teases him and leaves him dissatisfied. Sexual hunger makes his eyes bigger than his stomach.

> "HUSBANDS LIKEWISE DWELL WITH THEM WITH UNDERSTANDING...
> THAT YOUR PRAYERS MAY NOT BE HINDERED."
> I PETER 3:7, NKJV

Going around and looking at different women is never going to solve a guy's core problem. Love is not something a man finds in this world, it is something he makes. If a man really wants to experience a woman's love, He must make love to the woman first. A woman falls in love with a guy because she has been loved by him. Her sexual feelings are triggered by the man's own feelings for her. Before a woman will ever be sexually attracted to a man, she must feel those emotions emanating from him. Just as God endows men with the ability to implant his own seed within a woman and create life, He has empowered them to create love where none existed before. Learning to love like this is a part of becoming a man.

"TASTE AND SEE THAT THE LORD IS GOOD."
Ps 34:8, NIV

The ability to woe a woman comes from understanding Love's power of persuasion. Before a man can make a woman swoon, he must taste love's potency for himself. This means having personal encounter with the living God. The way a man seduces a woman closely resembles those same strategies God uses to win over the hearts of his chosen people. God entered the world to meet people at their own level. He embodied the very Love people were hungry for. He would show men His Love by living it out. In this way, people could feel and understand God's love. Though He had no physical comeliness that people might desire Him or material riches with which to influence anyone, God won the hearts of many people by giving them a Love they could feel for themselves. Before long, the women around Him were kissing his feet and singing His praises. Some of them would cling to Him and were unwilling to let Him go. The results of how God's Love has influenced the world speak for itself. The Life of Christ on earth has become the perfect example for a man to follow.

"And this is eternal life, that they may know You, the only true God..."
John 17:3, NKJV

A guy may think he already knows God from past religious experiences. But if He does not love God first and foremost, He really has no idea. For all those who truly know God fall in love with Him. Jesus said *"This is eternal life: that they may know [God]…"* Knowing refers to experiencing God's love on an intimate level. The term "know" speaks of an intimacy a husband would share with his wife. For a man to know God on this level, true Love must enter his existence. Real Love must come to live in a person. When God's love gets a hold of somebody, it awakens feelings inside just as any woman's sexual desires would awaken when a man loves her right.

MORAL RESTRAINT

WHY THE KEY TO A GREAT SEX LIFE

"... YOU DO NOT RECEIVE OUR WITNESS."
JOHN 3:11, NKJV

Learning to love begins with practicing God's ways and this means establishing moral boundaries for oneself. At first, the average guy will reject this instruction believing it will keep him from achieving any kind of sexual fulfillment. In his eyes, this commandment is perceived as an impediment to gaining one's desire. How does a man gain access to a woman by keeping himself from her? The man who thinks this is only looking at things from his own perspective. He is not seeing things from the woman's viewpoint. He doesn't appreciate how Godly restraint plays on a woman's psyche. Because the reverse psychology is not understood, the genius behind God's command goes unrecognized. If a guy could only see how Godly boundaries would help him win, he would feel different about it. For Godly boundaries are the key to winning with a woman and finding sexual fulfillment. The man who disobeys God's command can't visualize this payoff. Therefore, the lesson on moral restraint must be learned the hard way.

> "…'I WILL GO AFTER MY LOVERS'…THEREFORE BEHOLD, [GOD] WILL HEDGE UP YOUR WAY WITH THORNS…"
> HOSEA 2:5-6, NKJV

A man who goes off chasing every beautiful woman he sees will get nowhere. He won't respect a woman's boundaries. He will go right up to the strange woman sunbathing in a bikini on the beach and interrupt her time of leisure and relaxation. The man on a mission to get something always lack the presence of mind to stop. How would a woman perceive this behavior? The man's lack of control would look dangerous to her and this behavior would make her feel uncomfortable. She will always put the brakes on a guy who comes across as too eager or too aggressive. A woman will do this to protect herself. Please know if a guy refuses to control himself, he will never be able to win.

"FOR WHOEVER DESIRES TO SAVE HIS LIFE WILL LOSE IT..."
MT 16:25, NKJV

A guy who lacks self-control will always overdo it on the affection. Because he knows a woman wants to be loved, he will pour it on strong. This is a manipulation tactic; the man is hoping the affection will somehow win him sexual favors. He thinks more is somehow better. But a woman holds little interest in a guy who gives her everything. A woman will get bored

169

with a guy who lavishes her with attention; the undeserved affection will only be perceived as meaningless. These kinds of gestures will always go unappreciated. A woman will understand what the man is trying to do; she will recognize these kinds of gestures as a ruse. A guy who tries to manipulate a woman like this will only find himself manipulated. Smothering a woman with too much affection is the sure way to drive her away. Don't make it too easy for a woman. A woman will always do the bare minimum to get the male attention she craves. If a woman doesn't have to work for that attention, she won't.

"ALL THE MAN'S LABOR IS FOR HIS MOUTH..."
ECC 6:7, NKJV

A woman knows an overexcited male is only focused on getting what he wants. She understands that he does not care about her feelings and so she reacts accordingly. Love and

170

want are not the same thing. All men want but not all men care. A loving man cares about a woman's feelings just as much as he does his own; he restrains himself to make a woman feel comfortable. This kind of self-restraint is a hallmark of real love.

"[DON'T] MAKE FOR YOURSELVES A CARVED IMAGE
IN THE FORM OF ANY FIGURE:
THE LIKENESS OF MALE OR FEMALE."
DT 4:16. NKJV

A guy loses respect in a woman's eyes when he tries too hard or stoops too low. Pandering is a sign of desperation. A woman will look down on this type of behavior. She will lose interest in the guy who caters to her every whim. A woman is not attracted to an emotional pushover; she sees a guy who grovels as weak and needy. A woman is not attracted to weakness; she is attracted to power. Projecting manliness is way more important to a woman than being a people pleaser. A woman does not want to be idolized or put on a pedestal. She wants to look up to the man and not down. A woman is looking for a guy with manly qualities. Being strong is even more important than outward looks. A woman will always prefer a strong man to a pretty boy.

"THE WICKED MAKE THEMSELVES A STENCH AND BRING SHAME ON THEMSELVES."
PROV 13:5, NIV

When a guy lacks self-control, he loses that masculine aura. He starts whining and pining whenever things don't go his way. The little tantrums he throws for being rejected will only confirm for a woman she made the right decision. A woman wants a man and not a baby. A guy comes across like this because he is not controlling his feelings. He cries his heart out on social media because he is not getting the sex he wants. These emotional meltdowns makes him a

HOW MEN OVERCOME

social pariah to all the women who hear of it. A man should never be given to emotional outbursts. A real man remains in control by staying stoic and calm about the situation. The essence of masculinity is to be in control.

> "EVEN A FOOL IS COUNTED WISE WHEN HE HOLDS HIS PEACE. WHEN HE SHUTS HIS LIPS, HE IS CONSIDERED PERCEPTIVE."
> PROV 17:28, NKJV

The first thing a man must do is stop all the emotional bleeding. He must never use a woman as a tampon to bleed on. If he does this, a woman will only think of him as a woman and find it a turn-off. A woman has no interest in filling a man's spiritual hole. Understand moral compromise is what causes a guy's sexual success to slip away. If a man wants to win, he must get himself together. He must regain his spiritual composure. A guy needs to put aside the baby antics and become the man God called him to be.

173

The ability to steer toward a more desirable outcome comes from gaining control over oneself.

"DO NOT GIVE YOUR STRENGTH TO WOMEN, NOR YOUR WAYS TO THAT WHICH DESTROYS KINGS."
PROV 31:3, NKJV

Male restraint changes the dating game altogether. A guy who restrains himself no longer poses any danger to women. For he has shut off all the male affection making her afraid. A woman will stop running when she perceives the danger has passed. Her feelings about the guy will even begin to turn a corner. This is because the cost of feeling safe is to be ignored. Women hate being ignored. Male restraint causes a switch to go off in a woman's head. The woman's fear for her own safety will now give way to the fear of being ignored.

"...DO NOT SEEK A WIFE."
I COR 7:27, NKJV

A man does not realize starving a woman of attention is the best way to make her emotionally hungry. For all her playing hard to get, a woman still needs a man's love. A woman can't afford to let an admirer get over her and move on. The emotional deprivation causes her hormones to kick into overdrive. A woman's desire to be loved will make her aggressive. She starts chasing the guy and pining over him. This female commotion catches the attention of every other woman in the room; it sparks their interest as well and a snowball effect ensues. Now the guy is popular with all the ladies. He will find himself having to push away multiple women. This circumstance enables him to be selective. Why chase the opposite sex when a guy could have the opposite sex chasing him?

175

"...HAVE THE WISDOM TO SHOW RESTRAINT."
PROV 23:4, NIV

Why do women perceive a man who plays hard to get as high value? Because a woman only wants a guy who has eyes for her. She does not value a guy who chases every other girl around. To a woman, the man's ability to restrain himself is a virtue. A woman wants a relationship and not just a one-night fling. She wants a guy who can resist the temptations of other women. In her eyes, he is looking for something more. To procure such a man's affections, the woman also knows she will have to do more.

"...WHOEVER LOSES HIS LIFE FOR MY SAKE WILL
FIND IT."
MT 16:25, NKJV

The ability to exercise restraint gives a man
his power back. He can now lay down the law
because of his own take it or leave it attitude. The
willingness to walk away puts all the negotiating
cards in his hands. This ability commands respect
with women. A woman would feel powerful
when a guy would pine over her and lack all self-
control. She could play hard to get because she
knew the man wasn't going anywhere. His lack of
control gives her a sense of control over him.
These circumstances change when a man starts
exhibiting some self-control. When a guy cuts off
the attention without any explanation, he
becomes less predictable to a woman. What if he
does not find her interesting anymore? What if he
has moved on to someone younger and prettier?
These thoughts play on a woman's worst

insecurities. The man's aloof and distant behavior causes her to feel less wanted; it causes her to second guess everything. Moral restraint causes her to fall from her pedestal.

> "YOUR DESIRE SHALL BE FOR YOUR HUSBAND,
> AND HE SHALL RULE OVER YOU."
> GEN 3:16, NKJV

A guy doesn't want a woman playing hard to get. He doesn't want her to grow complacent or be demanding with him. He wants her aiming to please. Understand Godly restraint is how a man beats a woman at her own game. A woman will work hard to regain the foothold she had before. A woman will do almost anything to keep the good favor and attention of a man in control. If pleasuring the man is what it takes, she will do it. She will over sex the man just to secure his affection. She will acquiesce to his every whim. Loving restraint is how a man gets his way with a woman.

"THEREFORE, I HAVE DELIVERED HER INTO THE
HAND OF HER LOVERS...FOR WHOM SHE LUSTED."
EZEK 23:9, NKJV

A woman cannot help herself. She needs emotional security. These emotions override any reasoning powers a woman has. A woman can't go against her own nature. Women are drawn to power; they find the man who can exhibit self-control irresistible. The desire to seduce and control a guy is what makes her throb. The challenge of male restraint gets her juices flowing. The woman's obsession with being loved is what will make her the man's possession. Her desire to seduce him is what will enable him to take full advantage of her. Godly restraint is how a man gets what he wants. Understand less is more.

"A KIND MAN BENEFITS HIMSELF..."
PROV 11:17, NIV

At this point, an important clarification needs to be made. A man does not need to behave like a jerk to exhibit self-restraint. When it comes to the dating game, it just so happens jerks also come across as playing hard to get. Don't be confused by this coincidence. A woman likes a bad boy because he is bold and not really because he is bad. He expresses himself without any concern for her reaction; this makes him look like he is not desperate. Women are drawn to this kind of challenge and may even offer sexual favors to procure such a man's affection. Understand the positive outcome is created by the restraint and not the mistreatment. No woman wants to be mistreated. Any positive response she might offer for the behavior would be short lived. Being mean is a dumb strategy for winning the sexual favors of women. The strategy never works long term.

> "NOT RETURNING EVIL FOR EVIL OR REVILING FOR REVILING, BUT ON THE CONTRARY BLESSING, KNOWING THAT YOU WERE CALLED TO THIS, THAT YOU MAY INHERIT A BLESSING."
> I PETER 3:9, NKJV

Some guys might be tempted to mistreat a woman just for suffering a string of rejections. He would only look petty doing this. He would be demonstrating to everyone that he is a bad sport about the whole process. This would destroy his spiritual brand- the very aura of masculinity around him that would turn women on. It would prevent him from capitalizing on any positive response. Again, a man never wins by making a woman lose. For his own sake, the man must get over his sour feelings. Women are not really to blame for the man's failures in attracting the opposite sex. He was rejected because he failed to restrain himself. He suffered loss, experienced sexual frustration, and heartache because he disobeyed God.

> "FORGETTING THOSE THINGS WHICH ARE BEHIND AND REACHING FORWARD TO THOSE THINGS WHICH ARE AHEAD, I PRESS TOWARD THE GOAL FOR THE PRIZE OF THE UPWARD CALL OF GOD IN CHRIST JESUS."
> PHIL 3:13-14, NKJV

A guy doesn't really need to beat himself up about this either. Most guys learn this lesson of restraint the hard way because they don't want to restrain themselves. They try every other gimmick first. Compulsion must drive many of them to even try it. By the time a guy resorts to this tactic, he usually gives up in defeat. Every man must come to the end of himself. Suffering those losses put him in the mood to learn. Of course, a man could have spared himself a lot of needless heartache and loss had he learned this principle of restraint sooner. But every man must learn this

182

lesson at his own pace. For once a man realizes all his attempts at avoiding death were only preventing him from experiencing the resurrection, He would stop agonizing over the decision and begin relishing the task. The man's inward fear would give way to faith.

> "...THEY TRUSTED IN YOU AND WERE NOT ASHAMED."
> Ps 22:5, NKJV

For a woman to be with a man in the way he wants, she must be vulnerable. To give herself away like that, she must first believe in the man. She must believe that he will take care of her and keep her safe. She must also believe that he will always love her and provide for her. The number one issue women have with men is trust. Winning that trust will require being trustworthy. The man must really love the woman he is wooing. This means doing the right thing even when no one is looking. It is the man's goodness and love that keeps a woman coming back for more. The way a man cultivates a lasting relationship with a woman resembles those same strategies God employs with his people.

"... NO ONE PUTS NEW WINE INTO OLD WINESKINS; OR ELSE THE NEW WINE WILL BURST THE WINESKINS AND BE SPILLED, AND THE WINESKINS WILL BE RUINED."
LUKE 5:37, NKJV

The desire for fulfillment and life should be every man's motivation for righteousness. A man only hurts his own brand when he violates a woman's trust. He ruins the good relationship he has going. Contrary to popular belief, God gives a man boundaries for his own personal benefit and not his detriment. These boundaries help a man to hold on to the pleasure rather than hold it back. Godly boundaries can bottle up the pleasure like a fine wine to be preserved and savored. Fulfillment comes from hanging on to those pleasurable feelings and allowing them to accumulate. If one wants to have their cup filled, Godly boundaries must be preserved. Once a man discovers Godly boundaries are the secret toward gaining fulfillment, all desire to compromise those boundaries would be gone. Both the boundary and the fullness of joy from keeping it would be preserved.

INSPIRATION

FOR BECOMING A GOD SEND

"LIKE A LILY AMONG THORNS,
SO IS MY LOVE AMONG THE DAUGHTERS."
SONGS 2:2, NKJV

The sexual nympho is every man's wet dream. A guy will watch porn just to get a glimpse of her. A guy doesn't want a partner to have sex with him out of duty, coercion, sympathy, or guilt. He wants someone who is zealous and eager like the women on the screen; every guy wants a spirited lover like this. A guy may not know it, but procuring this kind of affection from the opposite sex is easier than one might think. The world abounds with women craving to be loved and within each one of them lies a dormant nympho waiting to emerge. In this way, God has already provided. He has fashioned the female sex to fulfill a man's wildest dreams. God has even left men instructions on how to realize this dream; tapping into the blessing is only a matter of learning how.

"[DAUGHTERS] WILL RUN AFTER YOU...
RIGHTLY DO THEY LOVE YOU."
SONGS 1:4, NKJV

Deep down every guy should know there is a formula for success. After all, some guys are just chic magnets; they attract women without even trying. As soon as the girls see such a guy, they flock to him. He sparks something within their imagination and lives in their head rent-free. That guy gets his pick of the litter. He can have anything he ever wanted from her. From the outside, this guy appears to have the magic touch.

An onlooker will often wonder what a woman sees in the guy she goes crazy over. Why are women are so drawn to these individuals? What is it about these individuals that creates such a magnetic pull? If a man only focuses on externals, the answer will remain an enigma. For most Casanovas are not considered the best-looking individuals; many of them don't possess a large wallet; and none of them cater to a woman's every whim. Based on these metrics, it is a wonder why these charismatic figures can impress any woman at all. No, something else attracts these women in droves- something about their personality.

"[SOME THINGS] ARE TOO WONDERFUL FOR ME...
[LIKE] THE WAY OF A MAN WITH A VIRGIN."
PROV 30:19, NKJV

Why is the Casanova so successful with women? He attracts rather than coerces. He knows that before a man could ever hope to play with a woman's body, he must first play with her emotions. Emotions influence women more than anything else. To make this physical connection with a woman, the man will first establish an emotional connection. He focuses all his efforts into the spiritual plane. The Spirit conjures all those emotions inside; emotions are manifested through the interplay of the spiritual and physical world. The Casanova will make it look easy because he is allowing those invisible forces to do all the heavy lifting. He doesn't get physical at first. He allows his Spirit to do all the chasing.

"...NOT BY MIGHT NOR BY POWER, BUT BY MY
SPIRIT,' SAYS THE LORD OF HOSTS."
ZECH 4:6, NKJV

The charismatic figure will let his spirit do all
the talking. Not so much through the divulgence
of words but rather through the expression of
feelings. A charismatic figure doesn't say he likes
a girl; he shows it in his behavior- show don't say
is the idea. He becomes transparent allowing his
real feelings to shine through. Owning one's
feelings is the most powerful thing a guy can do.
This strategy enables a charismatic figure to
accomplish amazing feats with women; feats the
average guy just can't seem to emulate or even
comprehend.

"LET HIM KISS ME WITH THE KISSES OF HIS MOUTH-
FOR YOUR LOVE IS BETTER THAN WINE."
SONGS 1:2, NKJV

Getting a woman with free will to do anything means making her want to do it. The Casanova does this by incorporating love into the dating ritual and the sexual act. Deep down every woman wants to be loved. Love gives a woman a little taste of heaven; the aroma is absolutely intoxicating to a woman. The sensations trigger a whole host of emotions inside. The effect leaves her awestruck and glowing. Wonder washes over her face and she becomes starry eyed. She will start looking at the loving man with those eyes; those sexy eyes which convey he is doing something for her. A woman does get wrapped up in these feelings. The sensations sweep her off her feet. For once a woman gets a taste of this love, she won't be able to get enough. She will keep coming back for more. To a woman, Love is better than any psychedelic drug.

"BECAUSE OF THE FRAGRANCE OF YOUR GOOD OINTMENTS, YOUR NAME IS OINTMENT POURED FORTH; THEREFORE, THE VIRGINS LOVE YOU. DRAW ME AWAY!.."
I SONGS 1:3-4, NKJV

Love is the ultimate aphrodisiac. Love weakens a woman's resolve to resist. To get more of that love, a woman will start letting the man have his way. She will have sex with him because her own burning desire gets the best of her. Understand what a woman wants deep inside does not conflict with what a man dreams about; her dreams are complementary to his. A woman wants more of that love inside for how it makes her feel. If a man embodies the kind of love a woman desires, she will want him inside her.

"I CHARGE YOU, O DAUGHTER OF JERUSALEM...
DO NOT STIR OR AWAKEN LOVE UNTIL IT
PLEASES."
SONGS 2:7, NKJV

Love awakens the nympho within. A woman cannot help herself; she is ruled by a desire to be loved. This desire holds dominion over her heart. Scripture says God grants the loving man authority over his partner's own body. A woman does not feel used in such a circumstance. She wants to be owned and used by her lover. She will want the man to take full advantage of her. Love makes sex on demand possible. The charismatic figure has come to understand it is not by might or willpower that a man wins, but only through Spirit. The way of a man with a maiden is a spiritual art. Understand the Spirit is the way.

> "A GOOD TREE CANNOT BEAR BAD FRUIT, NOR CAN A BAD TREE BEAR GOOD FRUIT."
> MT 7:18, NKJV

A lot of guys will try to walk this walk; they will try to fake it until they make it. This strategy never works; the loving persona cannot be faked. Male bravado is a tough boy act and everyone knows it. For whenever a guy puts on a false front, he puts out mixed signals. His words will say one thing, but his body language will say something else. His tone rings hollow. His actions lack conviction. All those staged mannerisms come across as self-conscious behavior. Something about the man's movements always expose his true feelings. True feelings cannot remain hidden. The man's true spirit fills the air around him. There are no short cuts. If man wants to really win with a woman, he must become that loving persona. Putting off the correct vibes always comes down to possessing the right Spirit.

> "FOR YOU HAVE HAD FIVE HUSBANDS, AND THE
> ONE WHOM YOU NOW HAVE
> IS NOT YOUR HUSBAND..."
> JOHN 4:18, NKJV

A woman can pick up on all the spiritual vibes a man gives off. She will be able to sense whether the guy is being himself or not. For she notices all those little things. She hears the spiritual tones behind the man's words. She can read the heart motives behind the man's deeds. Every little detail provides her with some emotional clue. If any conflicting messaging exists, it will tell a woman something is wrong. Those little revelations will flag a man's character and undermine his every gesture. To a woman, the spiritual wavelength is the most impactful form of communication. For she can know whether a man really loves her by his Spirit. The man's

Spirit characterizes his true nature. Understand the Spirit is the truth.

A woman yearns to find her prince. She waits in earnest expectation for him to come on to the scene. She is always on the lookout for a guy who embodies that kind of love she dreams about. She craves to see those passionate feelings inside a man (just as any man might crave to see what a woman would possess under her clothes). Painful hormonal yearnings cause her to groan inside for it. For a woman, the wait can be frustrating. A world of relational games has left her unfulfilled. Not just any warm body will do. A woman is looking for someone special; someone who will fit that loving persona in her mind. This is why a

196

woman finds herself drawn to those spiritual qualities. A woman wants the real deal.

> "WHOEVER SEEKS TO SAVE HIS LIFE WILL LOSE IT..."
> LUKE 17:33, NKJV

Unfortunately, the average guy will not answer this call. He is too afraid to be himself. He is worried about how a woman might react to his true feelings; he is afraid of being rejected. To spare himself these feelings of rejection, he won't even give a woman a chance to do it. Self-limiting beliefs keep him from even trying. Instead, he will try to sneak into a woman's inner circle of friends unannounced and unnoticed. He does this hoping to sway the woman's feelings into a more favorable direction. He won't want to look or feel stupid in front of the girl he likes, so he will overthink everything he does. His movements will not be fluid because he is trying too hard. Worry will cause him to hesitate and choke. The fear of loss causes him to look unsure of himself. This entire interaction doesn't feel natural. The guy comes across as someone trying to hide something. This all happens because the guy is not permitting the woman to choose. He is trying to control the outcome. His attempts at trying to control the relationship cause him to lose it.

"LOOKING UNTO JESUS, THE AUTHOR AND FINISHER OF OUR FAITH,
WHO FOR THE JOY THAT WAS SET BEFORE HIM ENDURED THE CROSS,
DESPISING THE SHAME..."
HEB 12:2, NKJV

The Casanova experiences a very different outcome because he has overcome his fear of rejection. He understands every man faces rejection at one time or another. No man is less of a person because some woman rejects him. Women reject men for lots of reasons. Many of these reasons are nothing personal. Being rejected is not the end of the world. A man may not be able to control whether a woman will reject him or not, but a man can always control how he handles that rejection. He can always choose to handle himself well.

"...BUT THE RIGHTEOUS ARE BOLD AS A LION."
PROV 28:1, NKJV

A guy doesn't have to feel bad or apologize for feeling the way he does about a woman. There is no dishonor in thinking a woman is beautiful or even wanting to make love to her. Real love is not a character flaw. A guy doesn't lose face in the eyes of a woman because of how he feels about her- his opinions and feelings do matter. In truth, Love is the highest compliment a man could ever pay to a woman. She won't forget the compliment- even if she rejects him for one reason or another. In truth, a man's love is his greatest asset.

*"Keep your mouth free of perversity;
keep corrupt talk far from your lips."*
Prov 4:24, NKJV

A man will only make himself look bad when he won't take no for an answer. If he starts throwing a fit over a woman's rejection, he will look like a baby. For only babies have an emotional meltdown when things don't go their way. A guy who does this kind of thing is allowing his feelings to burn out of control. He is proving to everyone around him that his feelings of love are just lust. For his own sake, he needs to stop doing these kinds of things. In the eyes of any woman, a guy doesn't want to lose his man card. He will never get it back. Those passions that are not tempered by any kind of moral restraint will only be viewed as a bad thing. A charismatic figure will never let his desire for a beautiful woman trump his manners. In terms of social etiquette, he is a law unto himself.

200

"BEHOLD, I STAND AT THE DOOR AND KNOCK."
REV 3:20, NKJV

A charismatic figure knows a woman must give her consent for any relationship to move forward. He understands every relationship is a two-way street. A woman will only run away if he does not respect her personal boundaries. Therefore, the charismatic man resigns himself into letting the woman choose. He doesn't worry about an outcome he can't control. He surrenders any thought of trying to sway the woman's opinion. Such a man has truly detached from the outcome.

"I PLANTED, APOLLOS WATERED, BUT GOD GAVE THE INCREASE."
I COR 3:6, NKJV

A charismatic figure understands time and space are needed for those loving feelings to develop in a woman. He provides adequate room for those sexual feelings to germinate. Restraint is a necessary part of the whole process. The skill of lovemaking resembles those same talents found within the agricultural profession of husbandry. In fact, the term "husband" derives from this profession. Love is cultivated in a woman just as any flower might be. A man simply implants the possibilities within a woman's mind and then withdraws to allow those emotional sentiments to take root. It is as simple as that. The wonder of love blooming into full expression is not a human work. A man must recognize God's role in the process and not interfere with it. Plant the seed, water it, and then allow God to do the rest. A woman's sexual passions will blossom all on their own. A man does not need to help God out with this part. Shine the love and then let God work the magic.

"...BUT WHOEVER LOSES HIS LIFE FOR MY SAKE WILL FIND IT."
MT 16:25, NKJV

The charismatic figure has figured out this process. He has undergone an emotional learning curve. He can now look a woman in the face and converse. He is calm and collect. He doesn't overthink things. He has stopped striving and entered the present moment. The willingness to let a woman go proves a guy can live without her-he is not desperate. In doing this, the man is demonstrating to everyone he has his emotional stuff together. The conviction of a man's heart gives him a relaxed physical frame. He is comfortable in his own skin. His spiritual composure allows him to play it cool. This kind of spiritual maturity separates the men from the boys.

A man who can stare rejection in the face and still project that loving air of confidence will demonstrate to everyone in the room he possess the greatest kind of personal charisma. Women find this kind of confidence stunning. To a woman, confidence is a very attractive spiritual quality. The ability to take rejection in stride and still be loving will stop a woman in her tracks and make her take a second look. A man who possess these kinds of spiritual qualities will find himself able to move mountains with a woman. For at it's core essence, male charisma is a love mingled with faith.

"ACCORDING TO YOUR FAITH LET IT BE TO YOU."
MT 9:29, NKJV

The charismatic figure is not afraid to own his feelings. He knows the effect Love has on a woman. His eyes can see right through her. He can tell she is turned on by seeing him turned on by her. This ability to see what is invisible gives him confidence. He is not overcome by a little resistance from a woman. He is not afraid of how she might initially react. The possibility of rejection does not deter him from being loving. The detachment from outcome enables him to express his affections without any fear of reprisal. By concentrating his gaze, he can set a woman's own passions ablaze. A charismatic man understands the kind of power he wields. This ability to project the right kind of Spirit at any time gains him an endless supply of sex.

"YOU ARE MY PRIVATE GARDEN, MY TREASURE, MY BRIDE, A SECLUDED SPRING, A HIDDEN FOUNTAIN."
SONGS 4:12, NLT

A guy does not need porn if he had his own personal nympho at home. For no man can outlast a woman in the bedroom. A woman's sexual longevity far surpasses any man's physical limits. She would be able to provide a man with more sex than he could possibly handle. She could suckle him until he couldn't take it anymore. A woman is a sexual fountain. God designed her to provide more than enough. The man who follows God's instruction will be able to drink to his heart's content; he will be kept over-sexed for a lifetime. Women are not the ones holding men back from achieving their dream. A woman's sexual motor could be started at any time. A man has only to turn on the love and let those desires permeate the room.

"...BUT I REFRAIN, LEST ANYONE SHOULD THINK OF ME ABOVE WHAT HE SEES ME TO BE OR HEARS FROM ME."
2 COR 12:6, NKJV

Learning to love is a part of becoming a man. It is the only hurdle that keeps a guy from getting what he wants. Man was made to reflect the image of God. He was designed to be that physical medium for God's love in this world. He was chosen as God's instrument to love some woman on His behalf. Each man is given this role to play. If a man chooses to fulfill that role, he will become a God send to a woman and will obtain everything he could ever desire from her. A woman is looking for Mr. Right. When she finds him, she will give him everything he could ever dream about.

> "...WHEN I BECAME A MAN, I PUT THE WAYS OF
> CHILDHOOD BEHIND ME."
> I COR 13:11, NIV

If a guy really wants to be 'the man', he must assume the persona. The title is earned by staying in character. Setting the inferior aside and becoming the man God calls someone to be. This personal transformation occurs after a guy has acquired the desire to do so- having learned to glory in God's process. Living the wet dream is the very pinnacle of manhood. A guy who achieves this state doesn't need to watch porn anymore. He has an endless supply of sex from his own woman. A woman does this because she loves being with her man. He has awakened the nympho within her. She brands him a God send and sings his praises to all the people around her. This feat wins him the respect of outsiders; they marvel at his prowess. Nothing else could ever validate one's manhood like this. A man enjoys this kind of glory because he does everything

208

right. My hope is that every man finds this true path and achieves this level of personal success. The Spirit-filled life is real living and following God's instructions are the only true path to achieving it. Understand the Spirit is Life.

"JESUS ANSWERED AND SAID TO HER, 'WHOEVER DRINKS OF THIS WATER WILL THIRST AGAIN, BUT WHOEVER DRINKS OF THE WATER THAT I SHALL GIVE HIM WILL NEVER THIRST...'"
JOHN 4:13-14, NKJV

"FOR THIS REASON, I BOW MY KNEES TO THE FATHER OF OUR LORD JESUS CHRIST...THAT HE WOULD GRANT YOU ...HIS SPIRIT IN THE INNER MAN, THAT CHRIST MAY DWELL IN YOUR HEARTS THROUGH FAITH; THAT YOU, BEING ROOTED AND GROUNDED IN LOVE, MAY BE ABLE TO COMPREHEND...THAT YOU MAY BE FILLED WITH ALL THE FULLNESS OF GOD."
EPHES 3:14-19, NKJV

REFERENCES

Anti Pornography.org. (n.d.). From http://antipornography.org

Bothe, B. T.-K. (2021). Are Sexual Functioning Problems associated with frequent pornography use and/or problematic pornography use? Results from a large community survey including males and females. Addictive Behaviors, 112. From https://doi.org/10.1016/j.addbeh.2020.106603

Bridges, A. J. (2010). Aggression and Sexual Behavior in Best Selling Pornography Videos: A Content Analysis Update. Violence Against Women, 16(10), 1065-1085. doi:10.1177/1077801210382866

Brubaker, L. &. (Producer). (2015). Snuff: A Documentary about Killing on Camera [Motion Picture].

Burke, J. G. (2000, Sept 30th). British Link to 'Snuff' Videos. The Gaurdian.

DeSousa, A. &. (2017). Neurobiology of Pornography Addiction- A Clinical Review. Telangana Journal of Psychiatry, 3(2), 66-70. doi:10.18231/2455-8559.2017.0016

Dines, G. (2011). Pornland: How Porn has highjacked our sexuality. Boston: Beacon Press.

Dorough, B. (Director). (2011). ABC News Prime Time: Young Women, Porn, and Profits [Motion Picture].

Fritz, N. M. (2020). A Descriptive Analysis of the Types, Targets, adn Relative Frequency of Agression in Mainstream Pornography. Archives of Sexual Behavior, 49(8), 3041-3053. From https://doi.org/10.1007/s10508-020-01773-0

Heather Wood, T. a. (2013). Internet Pornography and Paedophilia. Psychoanalytic Psychotherapy, 27.

Hilton, D. L. (2013). Pornography Addiction- a supranormal stimulus considered in the context of neuroplasticity. Socioaffective Neuroscience and Psychology, 3. From https://doi.org/10.3402/snp.v3i().20767

Jameson, J. (2010). How to Make Love like a Porn Star: A Cautionary Tale. IT Books.

Love, T. L. (2015). Neuroscience of Internet Pornography Addiction: A Review and Update. Behavioral Sciences , 388-433.

Paul, P. (2006). Pornified: How Porn is damaging our lives. Boston: St Martins Griffin.

Reportal, D. (2020). Digital 2020 Global Digital Overview. (No. 1). From https://www.slideshare.net/DataReportal/digital-2020-global-digital-overview-january-2020-vo1-226017535

Rothman, E. F. (2021). The Prevalence of Using Pornography for Information About How to have Sex: Findings from a Nationally Representative Survey of U.S. Adolescents and Young Adults. Archives of Sexual Behavior, 50(2), 629-646. From https://doi.org/10.1007/s10508-020-01877-7

Solano, I. E. (2020). Pornography Consumption, Modality and Function in a Large Internet Sample. Journal of Sex Research, 57(1), 92-103. From https://doi.org/10.1080/00224499.2018.1532488

Vera-Gray, F. M. (2021). Sexual Violence as a sexual script in mainstream online pornography. The British Journal of Criminology. doi:10.1093/bjc/azab035

Zhou, Y. L. (2021). Pornography Use, two forms of Dehumanization, and sexual aggression: Attitudes vs. Behaviors. Null, 1-20. From https://doi.org/10.1080/0092623X.2021.1923598

ABOUT THE AUTHOR

CHRIS TRAINER is a man who knows what it means to struggle with porn and overcome. The insights found within this book come from his own spiritual journey out of the habit. He tries to help other men make their own breakthrough by sharing his own thoughts and feelings about the process from the male perspective.

Did you enjoy this Book?

Please Share your thoughts and leave a Review.

www.ingramcontent.com/pod-product-compliance
Lightning Source LLC
Chambersburg PA
CBHW071933090426
42740CB00011B/1691